Models of Teaching Biology

Models of Teaching Biology

Dr. Ajitha Nayar K.

ANMOL PUBLICATIONS PVT. LTD.
NEW DELHI - 110 002 (INDIA)

ANMOL PUBLICATIONS PVT. LTD.
4374/4B, Ansari Road, Daryaganj
New Delhi - 110 002
Ph.: 23261597, 23278000
Visit us at: www.anmolpublications.com

Models of Teaching Biology

First Published, 2006

ISBN 81-261-2609-4

PRINTED IN INDIA

Published by J.L. Kumar for Anmol Publications Pvt. Ltd., New Delhi - 110 002 and Printed at Mehra Offset Press, Delhi.

Contents

Preface

The Models of Teaching Biology describes certain teaching models suitable for learning select topics in Biology. It also investigates the effectiveness of the developed models in enhancing levels of achievement, in realizing instructional objectives of learning Biology, in attaining educational outcomes and suitability in incorporating these to everyday classroom instruction taking into account the constraints of Time table schedules, teacher competency, examination system, syllabus etc.

The models developed were 'Discovery learning model,' 'Memory model' and 'computer based model'.The teaching and learning of Biology has immense possibilities of exploring diverse learning experiences so as to make classroom instruction interesting, relevant, pleasant and meaningful. The three models developed has potentialities in developing and effecting the instructional objectives of learning Biology and learning outcomes through diverse learning experiences. Discovery learning model takes into account the learning processes involved in scientific investigation. It looks at Science learning as a process of inquiry and engage students in scientific thinking. It involves active deliberation of the topic to be learnt and provides scope for classroom discourses enabling sharing of ideas, classroom discussion and whole class participation.

The Memory model was developed based on the memorization strategies proposed by Bruce Joyce and Marsh Weil in their book *Models of Teaching*. Memorization strategies are learning strategies that increase the student's learning skills. It develops independent study habits and promotes a sense of control to the learner. It enhances the capacity to store and retrieve information. In this context memorization strategies are relevant and it is necessary to equip students with various memorization strategies for effective learning. Computer based model exploits the capabilities of the computer as a learning tool. Building knowledge and developing abilities to meet the challenges and opportunities of the Technological age has become the major responsibilities of schools. In the wake of computerization the roles of schools are undergoing a sweeping change. Computers can enrich the learning environment and enhance the learning process. It makes education accessible and produce cost effective solutions imparting information. The incorporation of computers in classroom instructions can be made possible in learning of various subjects.

This book is based on a study conducted on a sample of 491 secondary school students of Standard VIII of different schools of Thiruvananthapuram district. There are 6 chapters. The chapter 1 deals with details regarding the different models of teaching, its relevance to the current educational scenario, the objectives of the study and the hypothesis formulated. Chapter 2 deals with the theoretical frameworks of the models developed. Chapter 3 gives a summary of the research studies conducted pertaining to Discovery learning model, memory model and computer based model. The methodological framework is summarized in chapter 4. The chapter 5 describes the details regarding the analysis of data and its interpretation. The major findings, discussion of results, implications of the study and suggestions for further research are highlighted in Chapter 6.

The present book is the outcome of the consistent help, guidance and counsel rendered by many people. I express my deepest sense of gratitude to my mentor Dr. Exemmal, J, Dean, Department of Education, University of Kerala whose constant guidance and help made much of the work possible. Personal communications with the following eminent professors Dr. C.P. Sreekantan Nair, Dr. T.K. Lalithabai, Dr. S. Sreedevi was a source of valuable insight in deriving the implications of the study. Dr T.K. Lalithabai spent much of her precious time in checking the conceptual clarity of the work.

I am also indebted to principals, headmasters/ headmistresses and teachers and students of the secondary schools in cooperating with the collection of data. I am extremely thankful to my friends, relatives and family members for their support and encouragement in completing the work.

Dr Ajitha Nayar K,
Principal,
St Thomas Training College,
Thiruvananthapuram-44.

1

Introduction

Education is a multifaceted process which encompasses the dual roles of teaching and learning. It is organized around four fundamental types of learning, learning to know, learning to do, learning to live together and learning to be (Delors; 1996). Acquiring knowledge and developing skills are stepping stones to achieving the ultimate aims of education.

Despite vast strides in teaching technologies, Classroom Instruction continues to be a vital means by which students acquire knowledge and receive information. Learning is a complicated process of selecting, interpreting, and integrating which begins when a person responds to a stimulus. Attempts to improve the quality and effectiveness of teaching and learning in schools must look into the understanding of what teachers and students do in classrooms (Abbott, 1997). Teachers play a significant role in each student's learning processes as the learning experiences provided by the teacher influence the quality of student's learning (Driver, 1986).

Learning strategies play an important role in reaching a wider audience in the classroom. The reality that a classroom comprises of students with diverse learning needs, interests and a wide ranging levels of prior knowledge questions the rationality of resorting to a single method in teaching /learning concepts embodied in the textbook. The teacher within the class is free to resort to any means that instills thinking, arouses the curiosity of the child and makes learning an interesting activity. Teaching process being the core of the educative process, new alternative strategies need to be developed and investigated, as conventional strategies have proved ineffective. But, however in spite of the freedom a teacher is given very few teachers resort to alternative teaching/ learning strategies in the classroom. Conventional approaches confined to lecturing and sometimes lecture-cum demonstrations becomes the part and parcel of the classroom learning process. This helps only make teaching boring, monotonous and oriented to content. Lecture Method has been found to be quite ineffectual in the realization of instructional objectives. In Lecture Method students are not involved actively in the learning process. Lecture Method has been criticized for its passiveness and undue emphasis to rote memorization.

Needless to say such methods help only the gifted or over-achievers. The main objective of learning science is to provide a systematic, practical and interdisciplinary overview of the discipline and to change student behavior through this knowledge.

Many attempts have been made to restructure learning strategies in science so as to make them more relevant to the concerns of the individual and to modern society. It is unfortunate, but true that the method employed for science teaching continues to be rote memorization, drill and practice. Conventional lecture method continues to be quite popular among secondary school teachers. Regarding the method of teaching, the Education Commission (1964-66) has stated **if science is poorly taught and badly learnt it is little more than burdening the mind with dead information and it could degenerate into a new superstition** (p. 76). The New Education Policy (1986) suggested measures to redesign the Science curriculum so as to make it related to life. It has been reported that the teaching of Science in countries like India are characterized by authoritarian teaching methods and rote learning (Baez, 1982).

Philosophers as well as educationists have deplored methods that emphasized rote memorization. In the 17th century Comenius advocated methods of teaching which made the subject interesting, appealing and relevant (Zaghlul, 1997). Rousseau in the 18th century condemned bookish and verbal mode of instruction which gave undue emphasis to **Words, Words and Words**. Pestalozzi in the mid 18th century emphasized the need for employing the best methods for teaching. Froebel also stressed on alternative teaching and learning strategies for making learning a pleasant experience. Froebel's philosophy was based on the principle that children learn best when they are engaged in the activity they like best. Therefore, play activities of children should be exploited for learning (Froebel, 1827). According to Dewey (1959) a proponent of Experential learning, Experiences provided are the building blocks of the process of learning. Meaningful Experiences provided makes learning effective. Information severed from thoughtful action is dead. A mind crushing load since it stimulates knowledge and thereby develops the poison of conceit. It is a powerful obstacle to further growth in the grace of intelligence (p 131).

It is important to try out new approaches in the quest for improving the quality of learning. Learning science aims at giving basic understanding and appreciation of scientific phenomenon—biological and physical. This will prepare the non-Scientist for a fuller and more complete life. Students need to be trained in the techniques of discovery and methods of acquiring knowledge through personal effort and initiative (Secondary Education Commission, 1952-53). The Education Commission (1964-66) emphasized the urgent need to raise the quality of science teaching to promote an ever deepening understanding of basic principles to develop problem solving, analytical thinking and to foster the spirit of inquiry and experimentation.

Teaching strategies play a significant role in enhancing the learning abilities of students. In the words of Gabel and Bunce (1994) Many of the Goals of science Education will be realized once teachers orient their teaching towards understanding of concepts. The New Education Policy (1986) stressed the need for relating science to everyday life. The Ramamurti Review Committee (1990) reviewed the National Policy on Education (1986) and emphasized Inquiry Teaching in Science. It is therefore important that teachers should be encouraged to adopt methods that contribute to meaningful attainment of concepts.

During the last few years there have been new developments in various components of curriculum at various levels. Educationists and curriculum planners developed and implemented various innovative programmes such as Models of Teaching and Learning for improving quality of teaching. Models of Teaching are different learning strategies designed to attain different educational outcomes in different educational situations. Joyce and Weil (1992, 1993) have consolidated and categorized the various Models of Teaching such as Memory Model, Concept Attainment Model and Information Processing Models. Models of teaching are actually models of learning, as these provide valuable insights to learners on **'how to learn'** (Eggen, 1986) These also help students to attain control of their own thinking processes thereby enhancing their aptitude to learn (Joyce and Weil, 1992; Joyce and Weil, 1994).

Jerome. S. Bruner, an American Psychologist is the most eloquent defender of learning by Discovery. According to Bruner (1965) Discovery Learning provides opportunities for students to explore their environment. Direct contact with the environment enables students to meet concrete problems that concern them and stimulates reflective thought and manipulation of knowledge. Modern science education is concerned with developing an inquiring mind. To develop this pupils should engage in free exploration and should provide opportunities for the development of various process skills such as Observation, Identification, Formulation and verification of hypotheses, Classification, Discrimination, Analysis, Interpretation, Experimentation, Prediction and Problem solving. Discovery Learning which helps to bring about an awareness of nature is also helpful in realizing the objectives of teaching Science. Learning outcomes become more meaningful when concepts are discovered rather than merely taught (Selberg, 1982).

The first advocate of discovery Learning was Socrates (1983). By a process of questions and answers known as Socratic Dialogue one discovers the answer by oneself. Rousseau's book **Emile** is the first clear description of discovery learning. In the word of Rousseau, **Let him know nothing because you have told him, but because he has learnt it for himself (p 111).** According to Dewey (1963) Discovery Learning provides opportunities for student participation and Learning by experiment. Teaching through mere verbal Instruction was discouraged. When students learn by discovery they are active and are provided diverse learning opportunities for different levels of students. In Discovery Learning goal is perceived, the pace is self – determined and learning becomes both self-sequenced and goal directed.

Lewin and Potter (1947) have reported that as **children get answers to questions by finding out their own routes to discovery, Students must be given opportunities for free exploration and should be given chances to participate actively in the learning process.** According to Anderson and Koutnit (1972) Environmental approach provides chances to apply text book knowledge in an interpretation of local phenomenon. Even though suitable outdoor resources are available to learn science through discovery method students are generally forced to memorize facts and principles without understanding meaning of terms, concepts and practical implications (Driver, 1993; Selberg, 1972; Wellington, 1983).

Studies conducted in the area of learning strategies have revealed that there is clear relation between one's learning abilities and the quality of the child's learning (Brown et al, 1983; Paris and Oka, 1988; Pressley and Elliott, 1988). Good teaching includes teaching students how to learn, how to remember, how to think and how to motivate themselves (Weinstein and Mayer, 1986). Students are expected to learn and remember considerable body of material. The process of teaching must be useful to develop various individual capabilities in students and will pave the way for meaningful and effective learning. Building knowledge and developing abilities to meet the challenges and opportunities of the Technological age has become the major responsibilities of schools. In the wake of computerization the roles schools assume have become wider in scope. Computers can enrich the learning environment and enhance the learning process. It makes education more widely available and produce cost effect solution to the dissemination of knowledge (Vaidyan, 1989). Computer integrated instruction is likely to emerge as a central goal for educators. Computer Assisted Instruction and Computer managed Instruction are intended to enhance the effectiveness of teaching (Numice, 1986). The integration of computer in a school is regarded as successful when computers are used in various subjects by a large proportion of students and teachers (Meister, 1984).

The ongoing Government policy to introduce innovation in the curriculum to facilitate learning has been welcomed by educators, teachers and parents alike. INTERNET has already been introduced in some schools on an experimental basis. This makes it extremely necessary to think of ways and means by which computers can be used as an effective learning tool.

Even though curriculum planners, educational experts and teachers are quite aware of the significance of the teaching/learning approaches like Discovery Learning Method and Computer-assisted Instruction due weightage to these are not given.

As a teacher educator, the investigator has visited many schools to evaluate teacher trainees and found that the majority of teachers are adopting Lecture Method for teaching Biology. This may be due to lack of practice and non-availability of suitable innovative models, literature and reference materials for using innovative approaches for the teaching /learning of Biology. It is presumed that a study of this type will be useful in collecting necessary data regarding various aspects of innovative models which in turn will be useful in the planning and preparation of suitable curriculum to make the Teaching/Learning process more effective and meaningful.

1.4 OBJECTIVES OF THE STUDY

1. To prepare Discovery Learning Model (DLM) on *Feeding Adaptations in birds,* Memory Model (MM) on *Characteristics of Planaria and* Computer-based Model (CBM) on *Cell Structure and Function*
2. To test the effectiveness of the developed models (DLM, MM, CBM) by comparing the achievement of Treatment Groups (Discovery Learning Group (DLG), Memory Method Group (MMG) and Computer-based Group (CBG) with that of Lecture Method Group (LMG) for Total sample in terms of

2.1 Pre-test scores

2.2 Immediate Post-test achievement scores

2.3 Delayed memory achievement scores

2.4 Extent of Forgetting Scores

3. To test the effectiveness of DLM, MM and CBM with regard to Immediate Post test achievement, Delayed Memory achievement and Extent of Forgetting scores for Sub samples based on following variables :

   3.1 Sex

   3.2 Locale

   3.3 Management of School

4. To test whether there was significant difference between High and Low Intelligence Groups (Students) with regard to Immediate Post test achievement (When the group was exposed to DLG)

5. To test whether there was significant difference between High and Low Intelligence Groups with regard to Immediate Post test achievement (When the group was exposed to MM)

6. To test the effectiveness of CBM, Self-Learning Method (SLM) and Lecture method (LM) using ANOVA.

7. To test the effectiveness of DLG, MM, CBM and LM in realizing the Instructional objectives included under the categories Knowledge (K), Understanding (U), Application (A), and Skill (S) for Total sample and Sub samples based on

   7.1 Sex

   7.2 Locale*

   7.2 Management of School

   * Note: *Schools of Rural areas did not have computer facilities at the time of investigation. Hence, Locale-*

wise comparison was not attempted for Computer Based Model

8. To test the effectiveness of the models DLM, MM, CBM and LM in attaining select Educational outcomes based on ratings of Experts and Teachers listed under the following dimensions
   - 8.1 Cognitive
   - 8.2 Affective
   - 8.3 Process skills
   - 8.4 Social interaction.
9. To study the effectiveness of the developed models Viz., DLM, MM and CBM for teaching Biology in secondary schools in terms of the following aspects:
   - 9.1 Availability of Resources for practicing the models viz., DLM, MM and CBM and Extent of practice of the models (DLM, MM and CBM) for teaching Biology
   - 9.2 Suitability of the developed models viz., DLG, MM and CBM for teaching Biology in secondary schools with regard to the following curricular aspects.
   - 9.2.1 Syllabus
   - 9.2.2 Time Table
   - 9.2.3 Examination
   - 9.2.4 Teacher Training
10. To identify the practical difficulties likely to be encountered by teachers while using the models at secondary level
11. To collect suggestions of teachers for the effective implementation of the models (DLM, MM and CBM)

2.2 HYPOTHESES

When the Treatment groups DLG and LMG are exposed to Experimental teaching (Total sample)

H1 There will be significant difference between DLG and LMG with regard to

1. Pre-test achievement
2. Immediate post test achievement
3. Delayed Memory achievement
4. Extent of Forgetting

When the Treatment group DLG was exposed to Experimental teaching (Total sample)

H2 There will be significant difference between Pre-test and Immediate Post test achievement

When DLG was exposed to Experimental Teaching **(based on Sub samples)**

H3 There will be significant difference in the Immediate Post test achievement with regard to

1. Sex
2. Locale
3. Management of School

H4 There will be significant difference in the Delayed Memory achievement with regard to

1. Sex
2. Locale
3. Management of School

H5 There will be significant difference in the Extent of Forgetting scores with regard to

1. Sex
2. Locale
3. Management of School

When DLG was exposed to Experimental teaching (Total sample)

H6 There will be significant difference between High and Low Intelligence groups with regard to Immediate Post test achievement.

When the Treatment groups MMG and LMG are exposed to Experimental teaching (Total sample)

H7 There will be significant difference between MMG and LMG with regard to

1. Pre-test achievement
2. Immediate post test achievement
3. Delayed Memory achievement
4. Extent of Forgetting

When the Treatment group MMG was exposed to Experimental teaching (Total sample)

H8 There will be significant difference between Pre-test and Immediate Post test achievement

When MMG was exposed to Experimental Teaching **(based on Sub samples)**

H9 There will be significant difference in the Immediate Post test achievement with regard to

1. Sex
2. Locale
3. Management of School

H10 There will be significant difference in the Delayed Memory achievement with regard to

1. Sex
2. Locale
3. Management of School

H11 There will be significant difference in the Extent of Forgetting scores with regard to

1. Sex
2. Locale
3. Management of School

When MMG was exposed to Experimental teaching (Total sample)

H12 There will be significant difference between High and Low Intelligence groups with regard to Immediate Post test achievement

When the Treatment groups CBG and LMG was exposed to Experimental teaching (Total sample)

H13 There will be significant difference between CBG and LMG with regard to

1. Pre-test achievement
2. Immediate post test achievement
3. Delayed Memory achievement
4. Extent of Forgetting

When the Treatment group CBG was exposed to Experimental teaching (Total sample)

H14 There will be significant difference between Pre-test and Immediate Post test achievement

When CBG was exposed to Experimental Teaching (based on Sub samples)

H15 There will be significant difference in the Immediate Post Test achievement with regard to

1. Sex
2. Management of School

H16 There will be significant difference in the Delayed Memory achievement with regard to

1. Sex
2. Management of School

H17 There will be significant difference in the Extent of Forgetting scores with regard to

1. Sex
2. Management of School

When the Treatment groups CBG, Self-Learning Group (SLG) and LMG are exposed to Experimental teaching (Total sample)

H 18 There will be significant difference among CBG, SLG and LMG with regard to Immediate Post test achievement

1.6 Scope and Limitations of the Study

The study was intended to develop models on Discovery Learning (Discovery Learning Model), Memorization (Memory Model) and Computer based Instruction (Computer based Model) to teach the respective topics *Feeding Adaptations in birds, Characteristics of Planaria* and *Cell structure and Function* at secondary level. The effectiveness of the models prepared by the investigator was tested by Experimental cum Survey Method. The suitability of the models in terms of existing curricular aspects and practical difficulties likely to be encountered by teachers while practicing Discovery Learning Method, Memory Method and Computer based method was ascertained using Survey Method. In spite of the necessary precautions taken certain limitations can be detected in the investigation. The following limitations have been identified,

1. The study was restricted itself to develop only three models viz., Discovery Learning Model, Memory Model and Computer-Based Model.
2. The Experimental part of the study was confined to a sample of 491 VIII standard students belonging to Thiruvananthapuram District. More generalized results could have been obtained by extending the study to other districts and increasing the sample as well.
3. An inter- group comparison of effectiveness of models selected for development could not be attempted as the topics selected for teaching each model was different.
4. The effectiveness of Computer based Model was tested on English Medium Students of Standard VIII as the Computer software was not available in Malayalam

1.7 Organization of Report

The report has been organized in the following order.

CHAPTER 1 was an introductory chapter which deals with the need and significance of the study, statement of the problem, definition of terms, objectives of the study, hypotheses formulated, followed by scope and limitations of the study.

CHAPTER II presents Theoretical background of various models of Teaching and theoretical frameworks of the developed models are explained in detail.

CHAPTER III Gives the details of various related studies conducted in the area under investigation.

CHAPTER IV describes the Methodology of the study and gives the details regarding the sample, Experimental Design and procedure, Tools and Techniques, collection of data and statistical techniques applied.

CHAPTER V presents details of the analysis of data, interpretation of the findings and discussion of results.

CHAPTER VI presents a short resume of the study, major conclusions, Educational Implications of the findings and suggestions for further research.

2

Theoretical Overview

In this chapter a brief outline of the theoretical frameworks of the models developed by the investigator are described. The models developed in this context have been adapted and modified from the models consolidated and generated by Joyce and Weil and have been given certain restructuring for effecting classroom implementation. The models were selected on the basis of practical utility, relevance and suitability to the learning of Biology. For the preparation of the respective models, the Investigator analyzed the Biology syllabus prescribed for secondary schools in Kerala and text Books, Hand Books, Resource Books and Supplementary Reading materials, Reference Books related to Methods of teaching and Models of Teaching.

2.3 Discovery Learning Model

Jerome. S. Bruner is the most eloquent defender of Discovery Learning. Discovery Learning Model has in recent years gained prominence as one of the most effective strategies in the Teaching /learning process. The Discovery Learning Model is a frequent description of modes of instruction that are contrasted with other forms of instruction called traditional, exposition, guided, didactic, teacher-centered, deductive or dogmatic (Shulman and Tamir: 1973)

The first advocate of discovery learning was probably

Socrates. In 1762 J.J Rousseau advocated a method of teaching which prescribed Let him know nothing because you have told him, but because he has learnt it for himself. The suggestion that a child's mental development occurs spontaneously, is part and parcel of his ideal of discovery learning. Discovery learning was a major focus of research and development during the curriculum reform movements of the 1960s.The Discovery learning approach was summarized in the book entitled *Process of Education* (Bruner:1960). Bruner is of opinion that any subject can be taught effectively in some intellectually honest form to any child at any stage of development (p 33). For this the content should be structured to enable understanding of fundamental principles.

According to Bruner (1960) the method of instruction should have the objective of leading the learner to discover for himself. The way of imparting knowledge is more important than the subject matter. The method of discovery can be acquired only through the practice of discovery. The method of discovery is a means to attain the end which is concept formation.

Concept formation is only possible when children become trained in concrete thinking. Concepts form the basic elements of human knowledge and the learning of concepts includes the cognitive processes of

1. Acquisition of newly encountered concepts
2. Elaboration of existing concepts
3. Development of cognitive strategies to employ concepts in previously encountered situations.

Knowing is a process not a product (Bruner, 1966, p 72). Teachers should emphasize teaching intellectual skills which includes abilities such as **observing, using space/time relationship, measuring, classifying, inferring, interpreting data and defining operationally.**

Bruner described the aim of teaching as

> We teach a subject not to produce little living libraries on that subject, but rather to get a student to think mathematically for himself, to consider matters as a historian does, to take part in the process of knowledge getting (1966, p.76)

Discovery learning refers to the unique individual experiment by which concepts evolve in the mind of the learner rather than being transmitted ready made. Discovery applies so long as a specific rule or generalization is not mentioned by a teacher. It is usually confined to hierarchically arranged subject matter in which the learner has considerable background. With instruction he has a fairly high probability of deriving by himself correct answers and generalizations (Wittrock: 1966).

2.12 Merits and Demerits of Discovery Learning

Many studies have been reported on the positive influences of Discovery method on achievement. Certain studies have revealed that Discovery Learning enhances intellectual potency of the students (Bruner,1966; Selim and Shrigley, 1983;Tamir and Goldminz, 1974). It has also been found that teaching through Discovery Method generates motivation, interest and satisfaction. Students were noted to develop a positive attitude towards science when this method was employed (Ajiwole, 1991; Mulapo and Fowler, 1987; Selim and Shrigley,1983).

There are also several criticisms leveled against Discovery Learning. Implementing Discovery method in schools with limited resources and in classrooms with a large student strength can be very taxing on teachers (Wellington, 1981). The basic model reported by Clark and Starr(1976) for conducting Discovery Learning consists of the following steps:

1. Select the generalization or generalizations
2. Set up a problem situation

3. Set up experiences that will bring out the essential elements such as problem solving, questions, demonstrations
4. Set up experiences that will bring contrasting elements
5. Draw generalizations or concepts
6. Apply the generalization or concept

2.13 Psychological Foundations —Discovery Learning Model

Discovery learning model is based on the principles of Discovery learning. The Discovery Learning model has in recent years gained prominence as one of the most effective strategies in teaching / learning process. Jerome. S. Bruner, an American Psychologist is the most eloquent defender of learning by discovery. According to him, discovery learning is usually initiated by presenting the learner with a perplexing situation or problem. Discovery begins when the learner senses an Incongruity. Bruner emphasizes the need for the learner to discover for himself solutions to the perplexing situation. The various steps included in the model are presented in a systematic manner under the following heads,

1. Observation of birds and classification based on structure of beak
2. Identification of structure of beak
3. Formulation and verification of hypotheses
4. Analysis
5. Interpretation
6. Discovering Relationship
7. Association
8. Discrimination
9. Structuring Models for representing various relations
10. Concept formation
11. Problem solving

The Discovery Learning Model prepared by the investigator on the topic *Feeding Adaptations of Birds.*

The Discovery method makes use of the processes like observing, generalizing, categorizing, inferring, concluding and predicting. It can be implemented through discussion as well as through explanations (Hyman, 1974).

2.2 Memory Model

> *The Memory model is specifically designed to increase the capacity to store and retrieve information. It should nurture a sense of intellectual power – a growing consciousness of the ability to master unfamiliar material as well as imagery skills and attention to one's learning environment. One of the most important outcomes of the model is the student's recognition that learning is not a mysterious, innate process over which they have no control.*

Memory Model makes use of learning strategies that help retention and immediate retrieval of content learned. Mnemonics are memory assists that provide the learner with easy and effective techniques to remember information to be learned. Mnemonics can be used in a large variety of contexts E.g., When new material is to be learnt, **when material is partly familiar, when content is similar but not related to another material already learnt etc.**

Effects of teaching depend on the Learner's prior knowledge and the learner's active cognitive processing (Anderson et al, 1977; Cook and Mayer, 1983; Dansereau:1985; Jones et al, 1985; Mayer,1984; Ryan,1981; Weinstein, 1975; Weinstein and Underwood, 1985; Wittrock, 1974, 1978). Goal of any learning strategy may be to effect the learner's motivational or affective state, or the way in which the learner selects, acquires, organizes or integrates new knowledge (Weinstein and Mayer,1986). Studies have reported that human beings have the ability to retain visual information. The integrative processes used by the learner to relate new information to either concepts or schemas already in semantic memory or distinctive memories of experience are the key determinants of new learning and subsequent performance (Wittrock, 1974,1978,1981).

Effective teaching includes teaching students how to learn, how to remember, how to think and how to motivate themselves (Weinstein and Mayer, 1986). It is strange that students are expected to learn and remember considerable body of material, yet seldom taught the art of memory (Norman, 1980).

Researchers have reported that young children can equal or outperform older ones when the content is something they know well E.g., **cartoon figures** (Lindberg, 1980), **names of classmates** (Bjorklund and Zeman, 1982), Soccer rules (Schneider, Korkel and Weinert:1987).

2.21 Mnemonic Strategies

Mnemonics represent schemes for helping to ensure the retention of material which would otherwise be forgotten. They range in complexity from the humble knot in the handkerchief up to complex or even mystical systems devised in the middle ages (Yates, 1966). A mnemonic strategy is any technique that people use in an attempt to help themselves remember something.

According to Bjorklund (1988) there are different types of memorization strategies:

1. Rehearsal strategies
2. Organization strategies,
3. Elaboration strategies

Dansereau and his colleagues have developed a technique called **networking** which trains students to identify the main internal connections among ideas in a passage (Dansereau,1978; Dansereau et al, 1979; Holley et al,1979). In the cognitive development of children. **Rehearsal learning strategies** which are simple are the first to be used by children. Organization appears somewhat later and elaboration later still(Bjorklund:1990). Learning of nonsense syllables becomes easy when each word is associated with another to form a pair. This is called Paired-associate learning. Meaningfulness of the syllables however influences the rate of learning (Cieutat, Stockwell and Noble:1958). Verbal material that has been processed in term of its meaning will generally be recalled better than material processed in terms of the letter structure or sound (Hyde and Jenkins: 1969). **Key or peg-word system** was introduced in England in the late 19th century by John Sambrook (Paivio,1979). In this a rhyme such as

one is a bun, two is a shoe, three is a tree

is used to associate an object (the key or pegword) with each number in the rhyme.The items to be remembered are then individually paired with a keyword by means of a mental image

---

If the first word to be remembered is a clock an image of a bun with a clock face might be formed.

Link-word method was first systematically studied by Atkinson (1975) and used extensively in the teaching of foreign languages (Gruneberg: 1992). The method involves initially constructing a concrete link word or words to represent the foreign word to be learned followed by a visual image to reinforce the link-word used.

The Greek word for a worm is *skooleekee*. This could be represented by 2 words which sound similar namely, **School** and **Leaky**

Reviewing and preparing questions on key concepts and issues are effective devices to remember information to be learned (Thomas and Robinson,1972).

In situations where new material is to be learned or content is familiar reviewing the text and attempting to answer questions will help in better retention.

According to Reder and Anderson (1990) those who read only the summary of the material remembered more than those who read the whole text. This was true when questions were taken directly from the text or required the combination of material and the drawing of inferences.

2.2.2 *Learning Strategies Facilitating Memory*

The information capabilities of adults and children are always limited. Only a limited amount of information can fit in short term memory. If new information can be rehearsed its lifetime can be extended considerably. If the child can think of categories and not individual items then much more can be retained. Much of the development consists of the creation of techniques to overcome information-processing limitations and thereby increase the power of the cognitive systems. Mnemonic strategies are a prime example of such techniques (Sieglar, 1991). Memory is aided by repetetion and association and improved by review (Callahan and Clark, 1980).

Learning strategies facilitating memory has been categorized into the following eight types:

Eight Categories of Learning Strategies

1. Basic Rehearsal Strategies

These involve repeating names of items in an ordered list. Flavell et al (1970) studied the spontaneous use of rehearsal learning strategies during learning and found it increased with age. Fourth graders encaged in repeating names of presented objects more than nursery school children. Similar studies have been reported by (Hagen and Kail:1973, Flavell et al (1966). Similarly, pupils who move their lips while learning had better retention than non-rehearsers. Rehearsal strategies are learned by children as they progress from nursery school to Vth grade (Flavell and Canizzo: 1967).

2. Complex Rehearsal Strategies

This comprise of startegies like copying, underlying or shadowing the material presented in class Rehearsal strategies help the learner to select and acquire information (Wittrock,1978).

3. Basic Elaboration Strategies

Forming a mental image or sentence relating the items in each pair for a paired associate list of words.

4. Elaboration Strategies

These are used for complex tasks—paraphrasing, summarizing and describing of how new information relates to existing knowledge.

5. Organizational Strategies for Basic Learning Tasks

Arrangement of content into groups or ordering items to be learnt from a list or a section of a prose.

6. Organizational Strategies for Complex Tasks

Outlining a passage or creating a hierarchy outlining assigned chapters in the textbook or creating a diagram to show the relationship among the various tasks in a structural design.

7. Comprehension Monitoring Strategies

These strategies comprise of self-questioning to check the understanding of material presented in class and using the question at the beginning of a section to guide one's reading behavior while studying a textbook.

8. Affective Strategies

Adopting certain mental states and temperaments can influence Learning. These involve being alert and relaxed to help overcome test anxiety. Studying in a quiet place and having a positive frame of mind, removing fear of failure, preventing thoughts of doing poorly etc.

2.2.3 *Merits and Demerits of Memory Model*

Many studies have reported the effectiveness of memorization strategies as a learning technique. Memorization strategies have been found to provide students with skills in thinking and recalling learnt material easily and effectively (Callahan and Clark, 1980; Norman,1980; Sieglar,1991; Weinstein and Mayer,1986). Mnemonic strategies have also found to improve the vocabulary skills of students (Beck,1982; Jones and Hall,1982). Certain memory assists like **Note-taking, Underlining key points, writing exercises and using key words** have revealed to enhance retention power of students (Arkes et al,1976; Atkinson, 1975; Barnett et al, 1981; Carrier and Titus,1981).

Using Mnemonics can also induce unhealthy learning habits among students like resorting to simplified and codified content, Learning by rote and retaining facts without adequate comprehension.

2.3 Computer-Based Model

Computer-based Model makes use of Computers as a learning tool in a number of ways. Computer-Assisted Instruction (CAI) is a natural outgrowth of the application of the principles of programmed learning. The main objective of programmed learning is to provide individualized instruction to meet the special need of individual learners. Use of computers in the school can be categorized into two types Computer –Assisted Instruction and Computer-Managed Instruction (CMI). In CAI students interact directly with computers. Computers can be programmed to introduce new material, ask puzzling questions and provide immediate knowledge of results. In CMI, computers are employed to help teachers plan, monitor student learning, analyze test results, schedule activities and store student records.

During the 20th century many attempts to penetrate schools with various technological innovations like OHP, Teaching machines, radio, 8mm film, TV, Video-Cassette recorders and computers. The majority of these did not achieve wide-spread use in schools and did not survive the initial years of enthusiasm. Some educationists see the computer as the key to realizing many hitherto unrealized educational goals such as promoting pupil-directed inquiry enhancing the development of scientific and mathematical concepts and addressing more efficiently the learning needs of individual children in mixed ability classrooms or those who are in need of remedial teaching. However, some teachers on the contrary point out that given the day to day demands of teaching most teachers do not have the time or skill to take advantage of the computer in the teaching of their particular subject

2.3.1 Steps in Developing a Computer Based Lesson

The steps involved in the development of a computer lesson are more or less same as the steps in the development of a programmed learning material. The main steps involved in the development of a computer based lesson are:

1. Planning of the Computer Based Lesson

Planning a computer based lesson involves making decisions about the following aspects:

1.1 Nature of the Audience

The age of the learners for whom the package is intended, the academic stream of the students, the medium of instruction are planned well in advance

1.2 Nature of the Topic

The topic is selected in such a way which has potential for paced, sequenced learning and use of illustrations to make the learning material appealing and motivating

1.3 Length of the Topic

The length of the topic is structured in such a way that it is neither too long not too short. Lengthy material may create monotony and too short materials may be inappropriate for classroom instruction.

1.4 Nature of the Program

The choice of the program is determined by factors like user-friendliness, opportunities for interactive learning and amount of visual/graphical presentations. The programming language should be publicly available with wide applications.

2. Preparation of a Computer Based Lesson

After planning the content and level of the audience, the computer-based lesson is ready for preparation. The following steps are involved (Collis, 1984)

2.1 Establishing Goals/Objectives of the lesson

The objectives of the planned computer-based lesson are

established. This determines the scope of the computer-based lesson, its structure, lay-out etc.

2.2 Structuring and Organizing the Lesson Pedagogically

The topic to be learnt is structured and organized in such a way to make each capsule compact. The learning material is prepared taking into account factors like prior knowledge and interest of the learner.

2.3 Writing the Program

The program should be written in a user friendly language which is content specific with appropriate means to teach. The program should be interactive and consider pedagogical aspects like interactivity, simplicity, readability and sensory appeal.

2.4 Editing

The program is edited to eliminate ambiguities, to sharpen and smoothen the program, to improve the technical accuracy and to examine appropriate use of figures

2.5 Testing

The program is tested for certain criteria based on content, teaching methods, instruction and presentation

2.6 Trying out the Program

The program is tried out and its effectiveness is assessed with respect to requirements with regard to the following:

(i) Program contents
(ii) Content presentation and arrangement of structure
(iii) Learner's motivation
(iv) Graphic presentation
(v) Essential elements of Educational Software

3. Types of Computer Based Instruction

Computer based Instruction comprise the use of Educational software to attain learning outcomes and realize instructional objectives in students. Educational software commonly used in computers can be classified into 3 types (Ellington et al, 1991).

3.1 Drill and practice,

3.2 Tutorial,

3.3 Simulation

3.1 Drill and Practice

Software belonging to this type allows learners to come in contact with facts, relationships, problems and vocabulary until the material is committed to memory. Students are asked a series of questions and students check their answers against the correct answers stored in the program. If the answer is correct a reward in the for of complement 'Very Good' or 'Excellent' is given. The pupil is presented with more questions. These are the simplest programs to write and the most commonly available. As a form of education these programs are usually monotonous (Preece & Jones, 1993). A majority of the commercially available computer-assisted instruction is in the drill-and–practice mode (Cohen,1983). The design of this mode is similar to Linear programmed learning. The drill and practice mode assumes that enough practice ultimately produces correct performance (Jonassen,1993).

3.2 Tutorial

The Tutorial type utilizes written explanations, descriptions, questions, problems and graphic illustrations for concept development much like a private tutor. Tutorial software is most effective when students show varying levels of conceptual understanding and it can provide for individual tutoring needs that may be difficult to satisfy through traditional instructional arrangements (Ellington et al, 1995). Tutorial courseware presents information taking into consideration individual differences on aspects of level of comprehension, background knowledge and information needs (Jonassen, 1993)

3.3 Simulation

Computer simulations are programs which stimulate real events. It is a representation of reality. This is an excellent mode which enables students to investigate and experiment with systems and processes which are complex, dangerous, undesirable expensive etc. (Preece and Jones, 1995).These attempts to answer "What would happen if " questions raised by students without taking too much of an already scheduled lesson plan. Computer simulations are not a panacea for learning. The simulation should be well-designed

Learning Sequence of a Computer Based Instruction

The Learning sequence of Computer based Instruction is as follows (Kemp and Smellie,1989)

$S_{(1)}$ Orientation Information

The teacher first gives an orientation to the students for the use of the computer program, Outlines the topic and presents verbally the objectives of the lesson

$S_{(2)}$ Directions and Procedures

The initial directions embodied in the software are read by the students. Students familiarize themselves with the learning procedure

$S_{(3)}$ Learning Procedure

Students read the textual information and observe the graphic displays

$S_{(4)}$ *Answering Questions*

Students answer the questions and test the realization of objectives included under the categories, Knowledge Understanding Application and Skill on the particular subunits of the topic

$S_{(5)}$ *Feedback*

Students obtained knowledge of results thereby immediate feedback is obtained

$S_{(6)}$ *Remedial Instructions*

Remedial instruction is provided whereby students are provided with supplementary information and references

$S_{(7)}$ *Choosing the Next Learning Sequence*

Students choose the direction of the learning procedure whereby they can go to a new unit, go back to the original unit or terminate the learning sequence by exiting from the program.

Merits and Demerits of Computer Based Learning

Computer-based Model plays a very important role in enriching the learning environment. It enhances the learning environment. It enhances the learning processes and produces cost-effective solution to dissemination of information (Reinking,1988; Vaidyan, 1989)Computer-mediated text improved level of comprehension of students (Reinking, 1988)Students taught through Computer-based Learning systems was found to perform better in achievement tests (Aguire, 1995; Chadwick & Holt, 1997; Chein, 1996;Defreize, 1997; Lee,1997; Lekshmi, 2001; MadhuMohan, 2000; Maya,1999; Swan, 1997; Renaud, 1997). Computers improved attitude of students towards subjects taught using Computer- Assisted Instruction (Jegede et al,- 1991; Nimmi, 1997) Computer-based teaching models provided scope for learner participation and catered to the needs of the individual learner (Ellington et al 1993).

The effectiveness of a Computer-based Model depends on effective software and appropriate hardware. Teachers may encounter difficulty in locating good software for a particular topic. Computer based Instruction requires a certain degree of computer literacy on the part of the students. It has been found to be not suitable for realizing higher-cognitive and non-cognitive objectives.

3

Review of Related Literature

The area under study has been inadequately investigated by Indian Educational Researchers. Some Academicians and various Educational groups have shown some sensitivity to this area. In India studies on Models of Teaching have gained momentum in the late 1980's.The research studies available are summarized and presented under the following heads:

1. Discovery Learning Model (DLM)
2. Memory Model (MM)
3. Computer- based Model (CBM)

3.1. Discovery Learning Model

Exemmal (1978) constructed models for teaching Botany using Environmental and Ethnic Resources based on the principles of Discovery Learning. The efficiency of the teaching models were tested by comparing the achievement of the Environmental approach (EA) group with the Formal approach group (FA) in terms of Immediate post-teaching achievement, Delayed memory achievement and Extent of forgetting scores.

The analysis of results revealed that Environmental approach group was significantly superior to Formal approach Group in terms of Immediate post test teaching, Delayed memory achievement and retention power. Andrews (1984) constructed models for comparing the effect of Expository and Discovery learning which is applicable to a wide range of environmental problems. The analysis of results revealed that the experimental group discussed low transportation and population issues to a significantly great extent than control group. With respect to realizing the objective 'application' the expository method was more effective than the guided discovery method for high intelligent group whereas the Low intelligent group performed better on 'application test items' when taught using Guided discovery method.

Bhalwarkar (1985) studied the effect of Expository and Guided discovery methods for teaching Mathematics on the Achievement of students for different levels of intelligence. A 2 x 3 Factorial design was used for the study. The data collected were analyzed using ANOVA and ANCOVA.
The study found that the Guided discovery and Expository methods were equally effective in realizing the objectives included under 'Knowledge' and 'Comprehension' dimensions with reference to both immediate post test as well as retention test. Mulapo and Fowler (1987) compared the outcomes of grade II students in Zambia for learning Chemistry by Discovery approach and their counterparts taught by traditional approach. Discovery approach was found to influence formal reasoners more than concrete reasoners which was evidenced by their higher test scores. The traditional approach resulted in higher achievement scores.

Rao and Raghavendra (1988) studied the relative effectiveness of Guided Discovery and Expository Approaches for teaching Mathematics. The major findings were

1. There was no significant difference between Guided and Expository group with regard to Mathematics.
2. There was no significant difference in achievement and problem solving skills in Mathematical concepts when taught by Guided and Expository approaches

3. There was no significant difference in problem solving when taught by Guided Discovery and Expository approaches.

Carole (1990) compared the effectiveness of Discovery instructional format on acquisition of concrete concepts for learners with and without prior knowledge. Learners who lacked prior knowledge fared poorly in the post-test when taught using Discovery Method. Passi et al (1984) studied the influence of strategy of training in 'models for teaching' for Teacher Educators. The study found that training in a particular model registered a significant favorable change in the reaction of teacher educators towards the model.Emex (1993) conducted a study on "The effects of guided Discovery style teaching and Graphic calculator use in Differential Calculus". Statistically significant difference were not found between the different treatment groups (graphic calculator, lecture, discussion and guided Discovery) style teaching.

Prema (1995) constructed and tested three Environmental –based Models for Teaching Botany at Degree level. One of the models constructed and tested was based on Discovery Learning Model. The study revealed that Discovery Learning Model was superior to Formal Approach in terms of Immediate Post-test achievement. Delayed Memory Achievement and Extent of Forgetting scores. The study also revealed that Environmental Approach was effective in stimulating cognitive aspects, developing affective behaviour, psychomotor skills in students. It was also found that Environmental resources were not being properly utilized for teaching/learning Botany at Degree level.

Byrne (1996) investigated the influence of Didactic and Guided method on recall of facts and comprehension. The analysis of data revealed that there was no significant difference between the groups taught using Didactic and Guided Discovery in the levels of Achievement.

Ambili (1997) constructed a Discovery learning model for teaching 'Sets' in Mathematics for Std VIII. The major objective of the study was to test the effectiveness of the Discovery Learning Method over Formal method in teaching Mathematics. The study revealed that Discovery Learning Model is more effective than Formal Approach in terms of achievement in Mathematics. The study also revealed that Discovery Learning Model is effective in the development of cognitive aspects, affective behaviour and process skills. Beena (1998) developed Discovery Learning Model (DLM) for teaching Biology at primary level. DLM was found to be more effective than Lecture Method (LM) in terms of Achievement and realization of certain educational outcomes included under Cognitive, Affective, Psychomotor, Social, Examination ànd Teacher competency dimensions.

3.2. Memory Model

Kenney et al (1967) studied the effectiveness of learning models based on spontaneous and induced verbal rehearsal. Students were required to recall a task and found that rehearsers who moved their lips while learning had better retention than non-rehearsers. The study suggested that rehearsal strategies are learned by children as they progress from Nursery School to Vth or VIIth or Grade. Shepard (1967) studied the recognition memory of Human beings for words, sentences and pictures and has reported that human beings have the ability to retain visual information.

Young (1971) developed a memory model based on link-word method for studying foreign languages. In this method a new word to be learned is linked to an old and familiar word. This method was found to be a highly effective mnemonic method. Hinzman and Summers (1973) developed a model based on visual imagery. Long-term visual traces of visually presented words were used. The study revealed that when presented words were shown in same or different case, subjects could recall the case in which items had been presented after presentation test intervals. The study also revealed that visual features of the stimulate are to some extent at least represented in memory and contribute to the recognition process. Atkinson (1975) constructed a model based on mnemotechnics in learning of second language. The study revealed that the method of using keywords enhanced performance in learning foreign language skills.

Raugh and Atkinson (1975) investigated the application of a memory model based on mnemonic keywords in the acquisition of a Spanish vocabulary for treatment groups trained and not trained in using Keywords. The study revealed that the experimental group was significantly superior to the control with regard to marks scored for the recall test. Another study by Atkinson and Raugh (1975) investigated the effect of a memory model based on keywords in the study of Russian vocabulary. The study revealed that students who used Key word method recalled 72% compared to 46% for the control group. Rickards and August (1975) studied the effect of underlining strategies on retention of content learnt. It was found that underlining important points of a passage ensured faster and easier recall of more information. Arkes et al (1976) studied the effects of orienting tasks on the retention of prose material. The study revealed that written exercises seemed to enhance factual recall. The experimental group was asked to copy a passage into their own handwriting while the control group did not take the written exercise. The experimental group remembered 50% more than control group. Bjorklund et al (1977) conducted a study on the impact of differences in organization of learned material on recall. The study revealed that subjects who grouped words on the basis of meaning showed greater recall than subjects who sorted in a random fashion. Doctorow et al (1978) conducted a study on the generative processes in reading comprehension and found that students who read a passage with inserted headings and who received instructions to generate summary sentences for each paragraph out performed other students.

Mayor (1980) tested the effectiveness of elaboration techniques and its impact on increasing the meaningfulness of the technical prose. The study revealed that students who answered elaboration questions performed better on tests of creative problem solving. Reder and Anderson (1980) studied the effectiveness of two learning strategies, one textual and the other summary to the text. The study revealed that those who read only the summary remembered more than those who read the whole text. Grant (1998) studied memory assists comprising of verbal and visual learning of science terminology by High School Biology students. An experimental group of 30 students were taught pictorially and a control group of 30 students were taught verbally. The two groups were equated for student profiles, learning styles Inventory and an embedded image test. Results indicated significant differences in outcomes between experimental and control group. Chen (1998) studied the effect of a mnemonic Keyword method on a foreign vocabulary learning task for adult learners with difference in verbal ability, learning style and trait anxiety. Individual difference in verbal ability Learning style and trait anxiety did not interact with keyword treatment and thus did not affect the effectiveness of Keyword method

Kimmel (1998) developed and evaluated a CAI science unit which was integrated with music as a mnemonic device. Students who took retest tended to be able to recall the content learnt one week before. Fifth grade students scored higher than sixth grade students. Students in Vth grade enjoyed the mnemonic strategy which comprised of the module integrated with music as a mnemonic strategy. Pfeiffer (1999) assessed the long term recall of elementary students using the keyword method. The Experimental group taught using keyword method was found to be significantly superior to the control group who received no training in use of keyword. Study conducted by Simon (1999) revealed that visual objects could help retention of lecture content. Visual objects were supplemented with preaching to adults in order to increase memory retention of sermon content The visual group was significantly superior to the control group in the retention test

Kuo- Newhour (2000) employed a single factor multiple treatment design to study the effectiveness of verbal mnemonics over visual mnemonics. A total of 111 IX nth and X nth graders were randomly assigned to 6 groups of different treatments. Results revealed that those who learnt through visual mnemonics excelled those who were taught using verbal mnemonics. Students who used experimenter supplied mnemonics fared better than who used self generated memory aids.

3.3 Computer-Based Model

Rosner (1989) developed and evaluated a computer – assisted model in basic electrical awareness which included 2 computer simulations and regular class room instruction from grades 6 to 9. It was found that content learning improved with grade level. Nachimuthu (1990) developed a learning model incorporating Computer – assisted Instruction on leaves for Std. IX and validated it to attain mastery level achievement. An overall performance improvement was revealed when taught through CAI. Jagede et al (1991) investigated the effects of computer based model on the attitudes and achievement in Biology of 64 students enrolled in a preparatory course for the Nigerian Joust Matriculate Examination in Biology. Following the pretest, students were randomly assigned to one of 3 Treatment groups-Individual use of computers, Co-operative learning mode and third group which received no computer instruction. The group that received computer instruction in the co-operative learning mode showed a more positive attitude towards Biology compared to the other two groups.

Burkman (1994) examined the relationship of individual learning style with achievement and attitude of students exposed to a learning model comprising instruction via two-way interactive TV. Pretest and post test were used to assess achievement gain score for both host and remote school students. Students of both schools registered a significant increase in Post test scores. Agarwal (1995) investigated the conceptual understanding attained by students exposed to different models of teaching viz., Computer Assisted Instruction, Programmed Instruction. The study found that Computer – Assisted Instruction was better for boys, students of higher Intelligence and students belonging to high SES group. For Concept teaching, the study revealed that CAI was more effective than Programmed Instruction (PI) method. The study also revealed that CAI was less time consuming for students than Programmed Instruction.

McClure (1996) conducted a study on Computer related Technology use in the High School Physics Classroom. The teacher planned and conducted a Teaching / Learning Model exposing students to a creative enjoyable introductory Physics program. Groups of students engaged actively in the learning process at a ratio of 3 students to 1 computer. The study revealed that computer related Technology use in the classroom freed the teacher from whole class instruction to concentrate on individuals and small groups. Brophy (1996) studied the effects of Hypermedia as a learning model on the comprehension of science text among sixth – grade students. It was found that the use of Hypermedia did not make a significant difference in the comprehension of a scientific principle. However, it was suggested that supplementary text could be used with Hypermedia to provide a more supportive environment.

Melozarek (1996) studied the effects of Computer assisted models on problem solving activities for learning Geometry. The results indicated that problem – solving activities using Dynamic Geometry computer software did not produce a direct effect on readiness for self directed learning. Swan (1997) developed a model and studied the impact of computer technology on student alternative conceptions and explanatory style. The study revealed that computer simulation registered a positive impact in improving conceptualization of abstract concepts like friction and gravity.

Schardt (1997) compared English language and reading skills of students with and without multimedia CD-Rom literature based – software. The experimental and control groups did not differ significantly in their English Language and reading skills.

Lee (1997) constructed a Teaching model based on animations and investigated the effect of animation as a tool for concept learning. One hundred and forty four, 5th graders were divided into 6 Treatment groups. The experimental group in which Animation was used reported significantly higher post test scores than control group.

Adamson (1997) investigated the impact of co-operative learning model with interactive multimedia and its effect on gender, attitude and interaction. The study revealed that student gender did not have a significant effect on either interaction or attitude in multimedia instruction. Study also revealed that students scored significantly higher than male students in their performance. Lafronza (1997) studied the interaction of adult learning styles for design of Learning models based on Computer Assisted Instruction. The effects of different software formats were examined on the learning process. The study revealed that cognitive style play a significant role in adult learners performance in CAI learning environment.

Joshi and Mahapatra (1997) studied the effectiveness of computer software in developing/prompting reasoning ability in science. The study found that students taught through the developed software package differed significantly from those taught through traditional method. The computer software was also effective in enhancing students capacity for analogy classification, deductive and inductive reasoning in Science. Crawford (1997) analyzed the effects of a learning style seminar and a model based on computer assisted Instructional package on the academic achievement of selected seminary students. The study found that students who undertook the learning style seminar as well as the computer – assisted Instructional model scored significantly higher than the control group. The student's – Academic Achievement was positively affected by utilization of computer – assisted instruction.

Batchelder (1997) studied the effects of computer – assisted Instructional model on achievement scores for Reading. Results indicated no significant difference between Treatment groups with regard to achievement in Reading when taught using Computer assisted instructional model. Hazel Baker (1997) examined the effects of alternative methods of teaching on Achievement in Mathematics and attitude towards Mathematics. Models were constructed for teaching Mathematics based on three learning modes viz., lecture, co-operative learning and computer – assisted instruction. Results indicated that students who participated in co-operative learning mode outperformed students in the computer – assisted class on post – test achievement scores.

A study was conducted by Allen (1997) on the effects of computer – based multi – media lecture model on community college microbiology students achievement, attitude and retention. The study found that the control and experimental group did not differ significantly with respect to Achievement. Students who took computer based multi – media lecture presentation group showed significantly more positive attitude towards learning Microbiology.

Moon (1997) designed and evaluated a model comprising of multimedia computer – assisted Instructional program related to understanding the mechanics of open Kinetic chain skills. The program was found to contribute significantly to students understanding of open kinetic chains skills.

Chadwick (1997) reviewed Computer–Assisted Instruction in Secondary School Mathematics class rooms. A meta – analysis indicated that computer Assisted Instruction was more effective than conventional Instruction for Secondary School Mathematics.

Shoffner (1998) studied the effects of Instructional Strategies on emerging technology – based visual literacy Instruction. The effects of varying instructional strategies on learning was examined. 138 undergraduate education students were randomly assigned to eight treatment groups and a control group. The levels of Achievement for the treatment groups viz., problem–based learning, networking, hypermedia-based instruction and co-operative learning Mode. Who underwent instructional strategies based on Problem solving, Networking, Hypermedia based instruction and Co-operative learning registered enhanced performance than control group where no learning strategy was employed.

Mach (1998) designed an hypertext as a teaching model and conducted a case study on student use of hypertext in an elementary school classroom. The study revealed that students can become effective users of book length expository hyper text with a minimum of training and practice. It also revealed that the attitude of students was influenced by task type and perception. Kin (1998) compared the effects of computer enhanced Instruction with traditional instruction on the learning outcomes of High School students in Anatomy classes.

The relationship between theories of learning style and student learning outcomes were also investigated. Regardless of Instruction received, the study revealed that Visually perceptive students scored higher than non visually perceptive students on post tests. Renaud (1998) developed computer based learning models and investigated the use of Computer – assisted Instruction in rural science education. The experimental group utilized a tutorial software program as an instructional supplement to their life science course. The control group did not use the tutorial software program but were allowed to interact with computers. The results showed that the Computer Assisted Tutorial program improved rural students science achievement. There was no significant difference in student attitude toward science or computer between both the groups.

Chien (1998) developed interactive computer – based model and, studied the effectiveness of interactive computer simulations on Engineering college students' conceptual understanding and problem solving ability related to circular motion. The study found that students using computer simulations had significantly higher scores than students not using computer simulations. Madhu Mohan (1999) studied the effectiveness of Computer assisted Learning (CAL), Self-study approach (ML) and Teacher –centered approach (TA) in the learning of Chemistry for Standard IX based on Post test achievement. CAL was found to be more effective than MA and TA. CAL was found to be equally effective for high and average Intelligence student groups.

Maya (1999) conducted a study to test the effectiveness of Computer assisted Instruction (CAI) in Biology for standard VIII. The main objective of the study was to compare the effectiveness of CAI, Modular Approach and Lecture Method (LM) in realizing certain select Educational Outcomes. It was found that CAI is significantly superior to LM with regard to

Immediate Post test achievement. The study also revealed that existing curricular factors are suitable for successful implementation of CAI.

Myers (1999) developed and evaluated a Computer multimedia software intended to explore applications in discrete Mathematics. The study found that class participation and student interaction enhanced after the implementation of computer lesson. Lekshmi (2000) conducted a study to test the effectiveness of Computer assisted lesson (CAI) on Genetics for Higher Secondary School students The main objectives of the study were to compare the effectiveness of CAI, Self Learning Method (SLM) and Lecture Method in realizing certain select Educational Outcomes. CAI was found to be significantly superior to Self learning Method and Lecture Method

Meera (2000) conducted a study to find out the relative effectiveness among different modes of Computer based Instruction in relation to students personality traits. There is significant difference among different modes of Computer based Instruction in realizing instructional objectives for learners with varying levels of personality traits. The investigator found that Drill and practice is the most effective and Tutorial mode is the least effective in enhancing the retention of what has been learnt. Rendell (2001) studied the effectiveness of a computer-based instruction program for remedial instruction in Algebra and Geometry. The post-test results revealed that the treatment group scored significantly higher than control group in terms of Numerical operations. Female participants were found to score significantly higher in Numerical operations than male participants.

Wendt (2001) examined two instructional methods for delivering a technical training course to sales people. The traditional classroom method of instructional delivery was compared with computer based training method of delivery administered using CD-ROM. The group that received Computer based instruction was significantly superior to control group with regard to Post test achievement. Vijayalekshmi (2001) studied the effectiveness of Computer Assisted Learning in Physics at the secondary school stage. The study revealed that Computer Assisted Learning was significantly superior to Lecture Method with respect to realizing Instructional objectives belonging to the categories Knowledge, Understanding, Application and Skill.

Conclusion

The literature reviewed points out the need for investigating the impact of Models of Teaching for Biology. Only limited studies have been reported in the area of Biology. Certain number of studies have been done on Discovery Learning model, yet their numbers are few when compared to those done on other Models of Teaching. Compared to conventional studies research studies on Memory models and Computer based Models are relatively few. Likewise the effectiveness of Memory Model in learning Biology has been under reported. Classroom contexts of implementing Memory Model has been cited vary sparsely.

4

Method and Procedure

4.0 Introduction

In the preceding chapter detailed description of Discovery Learning Model, Memory model and Computer based model was presented. In this chapter the methods and procedures of the study are discussed under the following heads :

1. Research Design
2. Sample
3. Tools
4. Learning Material
5. Collection of Data and
6. Statistical techniques

4.1 Research Design

In this study experimental control group pretest –posttest design was used in which

1. First two experimental variables for the four study conditions were the following:
   (A) Discovery Learning Method
   (B) Memory Method
   (C) Computer based Method
   (D) Lecture Method

2. The dependent variable was Achievement in Biology 4.1.1. Symbolic representation of the study Symbolic representation of the study is given below:

$G_1 T_1$ ______________ X_1 ______________ T_2

$G_2 T_1$ ______________ X_2 ______________ T_2

$G_3 T_1$ ______________ X_3 ______________ T_2

$G_4 T_1$ ______________ X_4 ______________ T_2

Where

G_1= Experimental Group 1 (Discovery Learning Group –DLG)

G_2 = Experimental Group 2 (Memory Method Group-MMG)

G_3= Experimental Group 3 (Computer based Group –CBG)

G_4 = Experimental Group 4 (Lecture Method Group-LMG)

X_1 = Treatment of Discovery Learning Method (DLM)

X_2 = Treatment of Memory Method (MM)

X_3 = Treatment of Computer Based Method (CBM)

X_4= Treatment of Lecture Method (LM)

T_1= Pre- test

T_2 = Post test

4.1.2 Stages of the Study

The study was carried out in three stages. First stage was the pre testing stage in which the learners were tested on intelligence and achievement.Second stage was treatment stage. The treatment was spread over three months covering one academic term. The four groups were taught the selected topics viz., *Feeding Adaptations* for G_1, *Characteristics of Planaria* for G_2, *Cell structure and function* for G_3. The control group G4 was taught all the three selected topics using Lecture method. The third stage was the stage of post testing. After the completion of experimental treatment the students were tested on achievement. The design of the study is presented in the following Table 1.

TABLE 1

Design of the Study

Stage	*Experimental Groups*	*Control Group*
Pre- testing	Measurement of students (i) Intelligence (ii) Achievement	Measurement of students (i) Intelligence (ii) Achievement
Treatment	Teaching Biology through Discovery Learning Method Teaching Biology through Memory Method Teaching Biology through Computer based Method	Teaching Biology through Lecture Method Teaching Biology through Lecture Method Teaching Biology through Lecture Method
Post testing	Measurement of students (i) Achievement in Biology	Measurement of students (i) Achievement in Biology

4.1.3 Variables of the Study

The study involved independent,dependent and controlled variables. The independent variables,dependent variables and the controlled variables used in the study are summarized in the following Table –2.

TABLE 2

Variables of the Study

Independent Variable	*Dependent variable*	*Controlled variables*
Methods of Teaching		
1. Discovery Learning Method	(1) Achievement	(i) Standard to be taught (ii) Subject to be taught (iii) Intelligence of student

2. Memory Method	(1) Achievement	(i) Standard to be taught (ii) Subject to be taught (iii) Intelligence of student
3. Computer based Method	(1) Achievement	(i) Standard to be taught (ii) Subject to be taught (iii) Intelligence of student
4. Lecture Method	(1) Achievement	(i) Standard to be taught (ii) Subject to be taught (iii) Intelligence of student

4.2 Sample Selected for the Study

The Sample comprised of 491 Secondary School children of Standard VIII from 9 secondary schools in Kerala. Due consideration was given to factors like Sex, Locale, Availability of infrastructural facilities etc, while selecting the sample.The students (N=491) was divided into four groups and taught through the four different methods viz., Discovery Learning Method, Memory Method, Computer based Method and Lecture Method. The Range of IQ was 85- 100 and the statistical analysis was done on the treatment groups whose Pre- test achievement scores were in the range 25- 38. This restricted the sample size for statistical analysis and follow up study to 210.

4.3 Tools Used for the Study

4.3.1 Discovery Learning Model to teach the topic *'Feeding Adaptations in Birds'* for standard VIII.

4.3.2 Memory Model to teach the topic *'Characteristics of Planaria'* for standard VIII.

4.3.3 Computer based Model to teach the topic *'Cell structure and function'* for standard VIII.

4.3.2 Achievement tests in Biology based on the topic selected for preparing the models

4.3.3 Judgement Schedule for Experts and Teachers to rate the effectiveness of the models developed viz.,

Discovery Learning Model Memory Model and Computer based Model.

4.3.4 Questionnaire for teachers to rate the suitability of the models developed viz., Discovery Learning Model Memory Model and Computer based Model for teaching Biology

4.15 The Kerala Non-Verbal Test of Intelligence. The details regarding the tools used for the study are given below:

(1) Models

The models were selected on the basis of practical utility, relevance and suitability to the learning of Biology. For the preparation of the respective models (DLM, MM and CBM), the investigator analyzed the Biology syllabus prescribed for secondary schools in Kerala, text Books, Hand Books, Resource Books and Supplementary reading materials, Reference Books related to Methods of teaching, Models of Teaching and Pedagogical principles were also analysed.

The details regarding the Models prepared by the investigator are given below:

(i) **Discovery Learning Model (DLM): Discovery Learning Model** is based on the principles of Discovery learning. The Discovery Learning model has in recent years gained prominence as one of the most effective strategies in teaching/learning process. Jerome. S. Bruner, an American Psychologist is the most eloquent defender of learning by discovery. According to him, discovery learning is usually initiated by presenting the learner with a perplexing situation or problem. Discovery begins when the learner senses an Incongruity. Bruner (1951) emphasizes the need for the learner to discover for himself solutions to the perplexing situation. The various steps included in the model are presented in a systematic manner under the following heads,

1. Observation of birds and classification based on structure of beak
2. Identification of structure of beak
3. Formulation and verification of hypotheses
4. Analysis
5. Interpretation
6. Discovering Relationship
7. Association
8. Discrimination
9. Structuring Models for representing various relations
10. Concept formation
11. Problem solving

According to Bruner (1965) Discovery learning provides learning opportunities to the learner to organize, classify information thereby helping him "how to learn. The Discovery method makes use of the processes like observing, generalizing, categorizing, inferring, concluding and predicting. Burner emphasizes the need for the learner to discover for himself. The way of imparting knowledge is more important that the subject matter". Bruner also asserts that the environment surrounding us is so diverse enabling us to discriminate many objects. To cope with the environment individuals engage in the process of categorizing. The Discovery Learning Model was prepared by the investigator on the topic *Feeding Adaptations of Birds*. The particular topic provides opportunities for numerous direct learning experiences, situations and activities.

(ii) Memory Model – MM

The Memory Model is specifically designed to increase the capacity to store and retrieve information.It nurtures a sense of intellectual power by imparting the ability to master unfamiliar material as well as imagery skills. Developing Memorization strategies involves the following steps:

1. Making students aware of the topic,
2. Structuring the information to be learnt
3. Linking information to familiar material
4. Linking information to visual representations
5. Linking information to associated information
6. Practicing the memorization strategy

The topic selected for constructing the memory model was *Characteristics of Lower organisms with special reference to Planaria.* It is a flatworm belonging to phylum 'Platyhelminthes'. It exhibits a large number of distinguishing characteristics as well as similar features which it shares with higher and lower organisms. Five Memorization strategies were used for teaching the particular topic viz., Use of Key words, Linking to Root words, building associations both familiar and unfamiliar and constructing visual representations.

(iii) Computer-Based Model

A Computer-based model is a learning strategy where classroom Instruction is supplemented with Computer based Instruction. The Computer is used as a learning tool. It imbibes the principles of Programmed Instruction. Students are provided opportunities to work at their own pace and are encouraged to learn by themselves. It embodies the concept of Individualized Instruction. Suitable measures are provided for immediate feedback, self evaluation and self- correction. The computer based model was prepared on the topic *Cell structure and Function.*

The content area was divided into 5 units. They are:

1. Introduction to cell
2. Cell shape and type
3. Structure of cell
4. Cell Organelles
5. Cell Nucleus

Each unit was classified into different capsules. Each capsule within a unit comprised of the following components:

1. Objectives
2. Key points
3. Introduction

4.14 *Achievement Tests in Biology Based on the Topics Selected for Preparing the Models*

To test the effectiveness of the prepared Models the investigator prepared three Achievement tests (T_1, T_2, T_3) based on the selected topics in Biology.

The Achievement Tests comprised of 50 items with a maximum marks of 50. Each item carried 1 mark. All the questions were of the objective type. Adequate representation to the instructional objectives **Knowledge, Understanding, Application and Skill** was given in the Achievement test.

4.16 *The Kerala Non-verbal Group Test of Intelligence*

The Kerala Non-verbal Group test of intelligence was used for the purpose of categorizing the students into High and Low Intelligence groups. The test comprised of Sections A-D. There were 12 Illustrations in each section. Each section was intended to assess the components of intelligence namely A.Figure Series B. Figure Classification C. Figure Analogy D. Figure Matrices.

4.15 *Judgement Schedule for Experts and Teachers*

The investigator prepared a Judgement Schedule to assess

the comparative effectiveness of the developed models for teaching the selected topic. It was administered to experts (N=10) and teachers (N= 90). For convenience the Educational Outcomes were classified under the following dimensions:

(i) Cognitive
(ii) Affective
(iii) Process Skills
(iv) Social

The Educational Outcomes were presented on a 5 point rating scale ranging from Very High to Very Low (VL) – Very High (VH), High (H), Medium (M), Low (L) and Very Low (VL). The validity of the Judgement schedule was ascertained using construct validity. The statements included in the schedule was based on theoretical principles of learning. Content validity was ensured by appropriate choice of items and by discussion with experts.

4.16 Questionnaire for Teachers

A questionnaire was administered for Teachers (N= 90) to rate the suitability of practicing the developed models at secondary level. While selecting the sample due weightage was given to variables like Sex, age, Management and Locality. Three major sections were included in the questionnaire Section I.

1. Extent of practicing the developed models and availability of Learning Resources for practicing the developed models
2. Suitability of the models with regard to existing curricular aspects:
   (i) Syllabus
   (ii) Time Table

(iii) Examination

(iv) Teacher Training

Section II comprised a list of Practical difficulties likely to be encountered by Secondary School Teachers while practicing the developed models.

Section III was meant for collecting suggestions from Secondary school teachers for successful implementation of developed models Judgement schedule was administered to Experts (N= 10) and Secondary school Teachers (N= 90). Questionnaire was administered to Teachers only (N = 90).

4.3 Experimental Design and Procedure Adopted

The experimental design adopted in the present investigation was Pre-test, Post-test, Parallel group design. The investigator selected students of standard VIII for the Experimental Teaching. (Groups were statistically matched on the basis of Intelligence and pre –test achievement scores).

4.32 Experimental Procedure

After selecting the schools for experimental study, the investigator made necessary arrangements with the Authorities of the Schools for conducting the Experimental Teaching. The Achievement test in Biology (Pre- test) and Intelligence Tests were administered to the Treatment groups Experiment Group 1- taught using Discovery Learning Method- (DLG), Experimental groups 2 (MMG) and Experimental group 3 (CBG).

4.33 Pre-testing

The Achievement Test on Feeding Adaptations of Birds (M_1) was administered to Experimental Group 1 (DLG, N= 60)) to assess the Entry behaviour of students of standard VIII.

1. Exposition to Experimental Teaching (DLM)

For conducting the Experimental treatment the Topic *Feeding Adaptations in Birds* was taught using Discovery Learning to the Experimental Group (N= 60) and the same topic was taught using Lecture Method to the control group (N=60)

Discovery learning exploits the inquisitive nature of students Children by themselves are curious and are capable of harboring ideas of their own. Discovery Learning enables students to pursue the path by themselves through the practice of Discovery. The concept of Feeding Adaptations of Birds were taught by giving direct learning Experiences. Students observed different types of birds. Ultimately through a process of inferring, predicting and problem solving students discover the concept of Adaptations.

2. Exposition to Lecture Method

The control group was exposed to the lecture Method which in essence is the regular classroom procedure. The selected topics were taught by the investigator systematically with the help of illustrations, charts and Models. Assignments and other Learning Activities were also given.

3. Exposition to Memory Method

The topic *'Characteristics of Planaria'* was taught using Memory Model to MMG (N = 60) and by Lecture Method to control group (N = 60). The Various memorization strategies like Key words, Linking to Root word, Association to both familiar and unfamiliar material and Visual Imageries were used for Experimental Teaching.

For implementing the Memory Model using Key words the whole content was simplified into a single keyword from which the content to be learnt could be easily retrieved. Thus all the general features of Planaria can be easily retrieved by recalling the term Planaria.

The meaning of the terms *Platyhelminthes* and Planaria were made meaningful by linking to Root words Platy= flat; Helminthes = worm. Another Memorization strategy involved Associating the content to be learnt to Familiar information (Learnt content). Students are familiar with the Digestive system of Man. Each part of the human digestive system is associated to its corresponding part found in the Planarian digestive system. A Visual Imagery was used to teach the Nervous system of Planaria. It was associated ridiculously to a *Ladder decorated with ribbons and having a wooden hand frame'*.

After familiarizing with the various memorization strategies students rehearse them in the classroom and apply these in other learning contexts.

4. Exposition to Experimental Teaching-CBM

For conducting the Experimental treatment four schools were selected which had computer facilities. The topic *Cell structure and Function* was taught to the control group using Lecture method.The Treatment Groups received Computer based Instruction (CBG) and Self Learning Material (SLG) based on the same topic.

Students were given exposure to computer lessons. The Computer Lesson was based on the topic *Cell structure and Function*. The key points of the content to be learned was presented. The content to be learned was introduced with general and contrasting features. The concept was presented with a brief description of Key terms and Illustrations were displayed wherever necessary. Students after completing a capsule went through a self-check, to get a self-assessment of their understanding of topic. Students were given opportunities to get knowledge of results. The grade obtained was made accessible to them. Immediate feedback was thus given. Students underwent remedial teaching if wrong answer was given and were allowed to repeat the question attempted wrongly. Provisions for enrichment was made available through assignments and list of selected activities which students took up

Exposition to Self Learning Material (SLM)

As part of experimental teaching students received self -Instructional material and were given freedom to complete the package within sufficient time.

Post-Testing

1. Immediate Post test

After completing the Experimental Teaching for Experimental Group 1, Experimental Group 2 and Experimental Group 3, the achievement test based on selected topics was administered to the three respective (three) Experimental Groups. (The achievement test used for Pre-testing was used for Post testing also). The Post test was used to assess Terminal behaviour.

2. Delayed Memory Test

To test the effectiveness of the model a Delayed Memory test was administered after 2 months of Experimental Teaching to assess the retention power (Extent of Forgetting) of students

The same achievement test was used to collect Extent of Forgetting scores for the three Experimental groups

4.4 Statistical Techniques Used

The investigator made use of the following statistical tests,

(i) Tests of significance for difference between means was used to test whether there is significant difference between the groups under study on Achievement in Biology

(ii) Analysis of Variance was used to test whether there is significant difference among the Treatment Groups (CBG, SLG and LMG),

(iii) Co-efficient of concordance was used to assess the degree of agreement among teachers with regard to the ranks assigned to the practical difficulties likely to be encountered by Secondary School teachers while using Discovery Learning Method, Memory Method and Computer based Method.

5

Presentation and Interpretation of Data

This section is intended to give details regarding the effectiveness of Models viz., Discovery Learning Model (DLM), Memory model (MM) and Computer based Model (CBM) by comparing the achievement scores of Experimental Groups [Discovery learning Group (DLG), Memory Method group (MMG), Computer based Group (CBG) and Lecture Method Group (LMG)] for Total sample and Sub samples based on the variables: **Sex, Locale and Management of school.**

The means and Standard Deviation of achievement test scores of the Treatment Groups were computed and the difference in means was tested for significance in terms of **Pre-test achievement, Immediate post-test achievement, Delayed Memory achievement** and **Extent of Forgetting scores.** The mean and standard deviation of the **Pre-test achievement scores, Immediate post-test achievement scores, Delayed Memory achievement scores** and **Extent of Forgetting scores** was computed for each of the treatment groups viz., DLG, MMG, CBG and LMG. The significance of the difference between means was calculated using t-test. The details of the analysis are given in Tables 1-12.

The details are given under appropriate heads:

5.1.0 Effect of Discovery Learning Method on Achievement

The effectiveness of Discovery learning method was investigated based on the performance of the experimental group (DLG) taught through discovery learning method on achievement tests conducted. The tenability of the following hypotheses were tested in this section:

H1 There will be significant difference between DLG and LMG with regard to

1. Pre-test achievement
2. Immediate post test achievement
3. Delayed Memory achievement
4. Extent of Forgetting

The details related to this hypothesis were analyzed employing tests of significance for between means. The results are presented in Table 1.

TABLE 1

Comparison of Achievement Scores of DLG and LMG (Total Sample)

Sl. no.	*Tests*	*Treatment groups*	*Mean*	*Standard Deviation*	*Critical Ratio*
1	Pre test achievement	LMG DLG	30.6 29.00	4.50 6.53	1.66 (Not Significant)
2	Immediate post test achievement	LMG DLG	35.92 29.3	5.92 5.4	6.4*
3	Delayed memory achievement	LMG DLG	26.58 20.85	7.1 4.3	5.3*
4	Extent of Forgetting	LMG DLG	10.1 111.2	2.5 2.2	2.5*

Statistical analysis of the data in Table 1 revealed that there is no significant difference between treatment groups

(DLG and LMG) with respect to Pre-test achievement scores C.R (60,60) =1.6;p>.05. The results indicated that the two groups are more or less similar with respect to Pre test achievements scores.

Hence the hypothesis formulated in this context $H1_{(1)}$ was rejected.

Analysis of results indicated that there was significant difference between Experimental and control groups with respect to Immediate post test achievement and Delayed memory test. It can be concluded that teaching through Discovery learning enhances the immediate post test achievement. This gain in achievement score is also reflected in the Delayed Memory test (retention test). This implies that discovery learning facilitates effective learning as content learnt can be recalled more easily and effectively. This result is supported by the Extent of Forgetting scores (difference between Immediate post achievement and Delayed memory achievement scores) which reveal a significantly higher mean score for the control group. This implies that the Extent of Forgetting was higher for the control group.

The hypotheses formulated in this context viz., $H1_{(2)}$, $H1_{(3)}$ and $H1_{(4)}$ were accepted.

5.1.1 Comparison of Pre-test and Immediate Post-test Achievement Scores–DLG

This section of the analysis tested the Hypothesis H2.

There will be significant difference between Pre-test and Immediate Post test achievement when the Treatment group DLG was exposed to Experimental teaching (Total sample). The results of the analysis is given in Table 2.

Details in Table 2 revealed that there was significant difference between the pre test and immediate post test achievement scores. The difference was in favour of immediate post test achievement. This implied that the Discovery learning method enhanced achievement in Biology. Hence the hypothesis formulated in this context H2 was accepted.

TABLE 2

Comparison of Pre-test and Immediate Post-test Achievement Scores of DLG

Tests	*Mean (M)*	*Standard Deviation (S.D)*	*Critical Ratio (C.R)*
Pre-test	29 (60)	6.5	6.1**
Immediate Post-test	35.9 (60)	5.9	

** Significant at .01 level

5.1.3 Comparison of Achievement Scores of DLG (Sub Samples)

The effect of the variables, Sex, Locale and management of school on achievement in Biology when students were taught through Discovery learning Method were analyzed in this section.

The hypotheses formulated in this context viz.,

H3 There will be significant difference in Immediate post test achievement, when the sub samples were compared based on

1. Sex
2. locale
3. Management of school

H4 There will be significant difference in Delayed memory achievement scores when the sub samples were compared based on

1. Sex
2. locale
3. Management of school

H5 There will be significant difference in Extent of forgetting scores when the sub samples were compared based on

1. Sex
2. locale
3. Management of school

The results of the analysis is given in Table 3

TABLE 3

Comparison of Achievement Scores of Sub Samples

Sl. No.	*Tests*	*Variables*	*Sub Samples*	*Mean*	*Standard Deviation*	*Critical Ratio*
1.	Immediate post test achievement	Sex	Boys	36.29	6.25	0.45
			Girls	35.59	5.61	
		Locale	Rural	36.83	4.88	0.99
			Urban	35.31	6.45	
		Management Of School	Government	37.30	5.39	2.08**
			Private	34.22	6.10	
2	Delayed memory achievement	Sex	Boys	24.89	6.89	1.65
			Girls	27.91	7.17	
		Locale	Rural	27.75	7.59	1.11
			Urban	25.67	6.81	
		Management Of School	Government	24.12	7.72	3.17**
			Private	29.41	5.15	
3	Extent of Forgetting	Sex	Boys	12.82	7.82	2.52*
			Girls	7.81	7.56	
		Locale	Rural	9.25	8.21	0.71
			Urban	10.75	7.95	
		Management Of School	Government	6.15	5.27	4.07**
			Private	13.42	8.45	

** Significant at .01 level * Significant at .05 level NS Not significant

Details in Table 3 revealed that there was no significant difference between boys and girls with respect to the Immediate post test and Delayed memory achievement scores. However, the retention power of girls was found to be better than boys when taught using Discovery learning. Students of Rural and Urban schools did not exhibit any significant difference with respect to Immediate post test achievement, Delayed memory achievement and Extent of Forgetting. It can be concluded that the achievement in Biology was not influenced by the locale of the school when taught through Discovery Learning Method. Students of Private schools were found to have better retention than students of Government schools when taught using Discovery Learning Method.

Regarding the tenability of hypotheses, $H3_{(1)}$, $H3_{(2)}$, $H4_{(1)}$, $H4_{(2)}$ $H5_{(1)}$ and H5(3) stands rejected. Whereas Hypotheses $H3_{(3)}$, $H4_{(3)}$ and $H5_{(2)}$ are accepted.

5.1.4 Effect of Intelligence on Immediate Post-Test Achievement of Discovery Learning Group

The hypotheses formulated in this context viz., There will be significant difference between high and low intelligence groups when taught through Discovery learning method was tested Details regarding the Immediate Post-test achievement (DLG) of High and Low Intelligence groups is given in Table 4.

The hypothesis formulated in this context viz., H6 was rejected as there was no significant difference between high and low intelligence groups when taught using Discovery learning method. This finding implied that Discovery learning method was equally beneficial to both high and low intelligence group.

TABLE 4

***t*-test Between Means of Immediate Post test Scores of High and Low Intelligence Groups: DLG (Total Sample)**

Treatment Groups	*Mean*	*Standard deviation*	*CR.*
High Intelligence Group	37.77	5.13	1.5 (NS)
Low Intelligence Group	34.85	6.27	

NS Not significant

5.2.1 Effect of Memory Method on Achievement

The effectiveness of Memory Method group was investigated based on the performance of the experimental group (MMG) taught using memorization strategies on achievement tests conducted. The tenability of the following hypotheses were tested in this section:

H7 There will be significant difference between MMG and LMG with regard to

1. Pre-test achievement
2. Immediate post test achievement
3. Delayed Memory achievement
4. Extent of Forgetting

The details related to this hypothesis were analyzed employing tests of significance for difference between means. The results are presented in Table 5.

TABLE 5

Comparison of Achievement Scores of MMG (Total Sample)

Sl. no.	*Tests*	*Treatment groups*	*Mean*	*Standard Deviation*	*Critical Ratio*
1.	Pre-test achievement scores	LMG MMG	28.77 30.42	6.3 7.6	1.8 (NS)
2.	Immediate post test achievement	LMG MMG	29.51 36.8	3.83 4.8	9.2 **
3.	Delayed memory achievement	LMG MMG	18.9 28.1	6.6 7.5	7.2 **
4.	Extent of Forgetting	LMG MMG	10.6 8.9	4.9 3.4	2.2 *

**Significant at .01 level * Significant at .05 level NS Not significant

Comparison of pre-test achievement scores revealed that there was no significant difference between the experimental group and control group before treatment which testified to the fact that the two groups were similar with regard to achievement in Biology. There was significant difference between Experimental and control groups with respect to Immediate post test achievement, Delayed memory test and Extent of Forgetting. It can be concluded that teaching through Memorization strategies enhances the immediate post test achievement, Delayed memory achievement and retention power among students. This implies that memorization strategies facilitates effective learning as content learnt can be recalled more easily and effectively.

The hypothesis formulated in this context viz., $H7_{(2)}$, $H7_{(3)}$ and $H7_{(4)}$ were accepted.

5.2.2 Comparison of Pre-test and Immediate Post-test Achievement Scores–MMG

This section of the analysis tested the Hypothesis H8.

There will be significant difference between Pre-test and Immediate Post test achievement when the Treatment group MMG was exposed to Experimental teaching (Total sample). The results of the analysis is given in Table 6.

TABLE 6

Comparison of Pre-test and Immediate Post-test Achievement Scores of MMG

Tests	*Mean (M)*	*Standard Deviation (S.D)*	*Critical Ratio (C.R.)*
Pre-test	28.13 (60)	5.3	9.3**
Immediate Post-test	36.8 (60)	4.8	

** Significant at .01 level

Details in Table 6 revealed that there was significant difference between the pre test and immediate post test achievement scores. The difference was in favour of immediate post test achievement. This implied that the Memory method enhanced achievement in Biology.

Hence the hypothesis formulated in this context H8 was rejected.

5.2.3 Comparison of Immediate Post-test Achievement Scores of Sub-Samples (MMG)

The effect of the variables, Sex, Locale and management of school on achievement in Biology when students were taught through Memorization strategies were analyzed in this section. The hypotheses formulated in this context viz.,

H9 There will be significant difference in Immediate post test achievement, when the sub samples were compared based on

1. Sex
2. locale
3. Management of school

H10 There will be significant difference in Delayed memory achievement scores when the sub samples were compared based on

1. Sex
2. locale
3. Management of school

H11 There will be significant difference in Extent of forgetting scores when the sub samples were compared based on

1. Sex
2. locale
3. Management of school

The results of the analysis is given in Table 7.

Details in Table 7 revealed that there was no significant difference between boys and girls with respect to the Immediate post test However, the Post test achievement of students of rural and Government schools were found to enhance when memorization strategies were used. The memorization strategies used were found to be effective more for Boys, students of Rural and government schools more than their counterparts. It can be concluded that the retention power in Biology was influenced by the variables Sex, Locale and

Management of the school when Memorization strategies were used.

TABLE 7

Comparison of Immediate Post Test Scores of Various Sub Samples When Using Memorization Strategies

Sl. No.	*Tests*	*Variables*	*Sub Samples*	*Mean*	*Standard Deviation*	*Critical Ratio*
1.	**Immediate post test achievement**	Sex	Boys	37.67	5.98	1.38
			Girls	35.97	3.10	(NS)
		Locale	Rural	38.29	4.45	1.99*
			Urban	35.83	4.84	
		Management Of School	Private	38.06	4.45	2..3*
			Government	35.83	4.84	
2.	**Delayed memory Achievement**	Sex	Boys	23.47	7.33	6.37**
			Girls	32.63	6.99	
		Locale	Rural	26.67	7.70	1.20
			Urban	28.97	6.99	(NS)
		Management Of School	Private	26.67	7.70	1.20
			Government	28.97	6.99	(NS)
3.	**Extent of Forgetting**	Sex	Boys	14.27	8.69	6.12**
			Girls	3.6	3.15	
		Locale	Rural	11.71	9.98	1.98*
			Urban	7.08	6.72	
		Management Of School	Private	6.41	7.3	2.17*
			Government	11	8.81	

** Significant at .01 level * Significant at .05 level NS Not significant

Regarding the tenability of hypotheses, $H9_{(1)}$, $H10_{(2)}$, $H10_{(3)}$, stands rejected. Whereas Hypotheses $H9_{(2)}$ $H9_{(3)}$, $H10_{(1)}$ were accepted.

5.2.4 Effect of Intelligence on Immediate Post Test Achievement of Memory Method Group

The hypotheses formulated in this context viz., There will be significant difference between high and low intelligence groups when taught using memorization strategies was tested. Details regarding the Immediate Post-test achievement (MMG) of High and Low Intelligence groups is given in Table 8.

TABLE 8

***t*-test Between Means of Immediate Post Test Scores of High and Low Intelligence Groups: MMG (Total Sample)**

Treatment Groups	*Mean*	*Standard deviation*	*CR.*
High Intelligence Group	36.25	5.47	
			0.52
Low Intelligence Group	37.11	5.16	

NS –Not significant

The hypothesis formulated in this context viz., H12 was rejected as there was no significant difference between high and low intelligence groups when taught using memorization strategies.

5.3.1 Effect of Computer Based Method on Achievement

The effectiveness of Computer based method on achievement was investigated based on the performance of the experimental group (CBG) taught through computer based method on achievement tests conducted. The tenability of the following hypotheses were tested in this section:

H1 There will be significant difference between CBG(N=30) and LMG(N=60) with regard to

1. Pre-test achievement
2. Immediate post test achievement
3. Delayed Memory achievement
4. Extent of Forgetting.

The details related to this hypothesis were ınalyzed

employing tests of significance for difference between means. The results are presented in Table 9.

TABLE 9

Comparison of Achievement Scores of Computer Based Group and Lecture Method Group (Total Sample)

Sl. no.	*Tests*	*Treatment groups*	*Mean*	*Standard Deviation*	*Critical Ratio*
1.	Pre-test achievement test	LMG	32.8 (N=30)	6.7	1.8
		CBG	30.7 (N=60)	4.5	(NS)
2.	Immediate post test achievement	LMG	26.93	3.52	8.8**
		CBG	36.6	5.53	
3.	Delayed memory achievement	LMG	21.3	4.64	9.4**
		CBG	32.0	5.3	
4.	Extent of Forgetting	LMG	6.23	3.67	1.96*
		CBG	4.6	3.8	

** Significant at .01 level * Significant at .05 level NS –Not significant

Analysis of results indicated that there was no significant difference between Experimental and control groups with respect to Pre-test achievement. Thus Hypothesis $H13_{(1)}$ was rejected Results revealed that there was significant difference between Experimental and control groups with respect to Immediate post test achievement, Delayed memory test and Extent of Forgetting.

The hypothesis formulated in this context viz., $H13_{(2)}$, $H13_{(3)}$ and $H13_{(4)}$ were accepted.

5.3.2 Comparison of Pre-test and Immediate Post-test Achievement Scores–CBG

This section of the analysis tested the Hypothesis H14

There will be significant difference between Pre-test and Immediate Post test achievement when the Treatment group CBG was exposed to Experimental teaching (Total sample). The results of the analysis is given in Table 10.

TABLE 10

Comparison of Pre-test and Immediate Post-test Achievement Scores of CBG

Tests	*Mean (M)*	*Standard Deviation (S.D)*	*Critical Ratio (C.R.)*
Pre-test	30.7 (30)	4.5	5.4**
Immediate Post-test	36.6 (30)	5.5	

** Significant at .01 level

Details in Table 10 revealed that there was significant difference between the pre test and immediate post test achievement scores. The difference was in favour of immediate post test achievement. This implied that the Computer based method enhanced achievement in Biology.

Hence the hypothesis formulated in this context H14 was accepted.

5.3.3 Comparison of Achievement Scores of CBG (Sub Samples)

The effect of the variables, Sex, Locale and management of school on achievement in Biology when students were taught through Computer based Method were analyzed in this section. The hypotheses formulated in this context viz.,

H15 There will be significant difference in Immediate post test achievement, when the sub samples were compared based on

1. Sex
2. Management of school

H16 There will be significant difference in Delayed memory achievement scores when the sub samples were compared based on

1. Sex
2. Management of school.

H17 There will be significant difference in Extent of forgetting scores when the sub samples were compared based on.

1. Sex
2. Management of school

The results of the analysis is given in Table 11.

TABLE 11

Comparison of Immediate Post Test Scores of Various Sub Samples When Using Computer Based Method

Sl. No.	*Tests*	*Variables*	*Sub Samples*	*Mean*	*Standard Deviation*	*Critical Ratio*
1.	**Immediate post test achievement**	Sex	Boys	36.43	2.64	5.2**
			Girls	39.62	2.42	
		Management of School	Government	38.83	1.54	3.7**
			Private	40.68	1.96	
2	**Delayed memory Achievement**	Sex	Boys	28.26	2.21	3.42**
			Girls	30.13	2.93	
		Management of School	Government	36.23	2.21	2.47**
			Private	34.34	2.93	
3	**Extent of Forgetting**	Sex	Boys	8.17	1.78	1.57
			Girls	9.49	2.21	
		Management of School	Government	2.60	1.23	
			Private	6.34	2.30	2.12**

** Significant at .01 level NS Not significant

* Significant at .05 level

Details in Table 11 revealed that there was significant difference between boys and girls; and students of Government and private schools with respect to the Immediate post test when students were taught using computer based method. The differences were in favor of Girls and students of private schools. It is also evident from Table 11 that there was significant difference between boys and girls; and students of Government and private schools with respect to the Delayed Memory test. The differences were in favour of Girls and students of Government schools.

Regarding the tenability of hypotheses, H17(1), stands rejected. Whereas Hypotheses $H15_{(1)}$, $H15_{(2)}$, $H16_{(1)}$ and $H16_{(2)}$ are accepted.

5.3.4 Comparison of Treatment Groups – CBG, SLG and LMG

This section of the analysis gives the details about the comparative effectiveness of Computer based Group (CBG), Self Learning Group (SLG) and Lecture Method Group (LMG) in terms of Immediate Post-test achievement scores. Analysis of variance was used to see whether the groups differ with regard to Immediate Post-test achievement. Results of the analysis is given in Table 12.

TABLE 12

Summary of ANOVA

Source of variation	*SS*	*df*	M_{sx}	*F*
Between	12045	2	6023	
Within groups	186882	87	2148	2.8

F (2,87) = 2.8; p<.01

It is evident from the Table 12 that there is significant difference between the treatment groups CBG, SIG and LMG with respect to Immediate post test achievement scores. The F-ratios obtained was found to be significant at .01 level

F (2,87)= 2.8; $p < .01$. The significant value obtained warranted the follow up computations comprising of Covariance Analysis.

The sum of scores, mean scores variances and F-ratio for the Pre-test and Immediate Post-test scores of CBG, SLG and LMG were calculated. The details of the analysis is given in Table 13.

TABLE 13

Summary of Ancova

Source of variation	*SS*	*df*	M_{sx}	*F*
Between	19497	2	9748	
Within groups	169064	87	1943	5.01

F (2,87) = 5.01; $p<.01$

F at .05 = 1.99

F at .01 = 2.64

The obtained value of F-ratio is 5.01 and is greater than the Table value at .01 level and is significant F (2,87) = 5.01,$p<.01$. The results reveals that there is significant difference in Immediate Post test achievement scores among CBG, SLG and LMG after they have been adjusted for difference in the Immediate Post test scores.The F-ratio indicates that the three groups differ but do not indicate which group is superior. This warrants a follow-up analysis. The adjusted means for the Immediate Post test scores of the three treatment groups was computed using correlation and regression. Details of the analysis is given in Table 14.

It is evident from Table 14 that CBM ($My.x$ = 36.11) is superior to both SLM ($My.x$ = 29.8) and LM ($My.x$ = 30.05) with respect to Immediate Post-test achievement.

Results in Table 16 reveal that level of achievement in Biology when students are taught through computer based method is enhanced the maximum followed next by lecture method. Enhancement of levels of achievement is least for Self learning instruction.

TABLE 14

Adjusted Means for the Immediate Post-test Achievement Scores

Source of variation	*N*	*Mx*	*My*	*My.x*
COM	30	30.22	31.5	36.11
SLM	30	26.9	27.7	29.8
LM	60	27.12	36.6	30.05

From Table D for df

F at .05 = 1.97 *F* at .01 = 2.59

5.4 Realization of Instructional Objectives When Taught Using Discovery Learning Method, Memorization Strategies and Computer Based Method

This section is intended to give details regarding the effectiveness of Models viz., Discovery Learning Model (DLM), Memory model (MM) and computer based model (CBM) in realizing instructional objectives belonging to categories Knowledge, Understanding, Application and Skill by comparing the post test achievement scores of Experimental Groups and Control groups for Total sample. Comparison of sub samples based on the variables: **Sex, Locale and Management of school** was also attempted.

The means and Standard Deviation of achievement test scores of the Treatment Groups were computed and the difference in means was tested for significance in terms of **Immediate post test achievement**. The significance of the difference between means was calculated using t-test. The details of the analysis are given in Tables 15-20.

The details are given under appropriate heads:

TABLE 15

t-test Between Means of Immediate Post Test Scores of DLG and LMG - Realization of Instructional Objective (Total Sample)

Instructional Objective	*Mean (M)*		*Standard Deviation (S.D)*		*Critical Ratio (CR)*
	DLM	*LM*	*DLM*	*LM*	
K	10.6	8.1	5.9	2.0	3.1**
U	16.1	10.89	5.4	4.00	6.0**
A	5.35	4.41	1.1	1.8	3.4**
S	4.1	5.9	1.6	1.5	6.3**

** Significant at .01 level

Details from Table 15 revealed that there was significant difference between Lecture method and Discovery Learning Method with respect to realization of instructional objectives belonging to the categories Knowledge, Understanding, Application and Skill. The differences were in favour of Discovery Learning Method.

TABLE 16

Realization of Instructional Objectives When Students are Taught Through Discovery

Sl. No.	*Instructional Objectives*	*Variables*	*Sub Samples*	*Mean*	*Standard Deviation*	*Critical Ratio*
1.	Knowledge	Sex	Boys	10.31	2.44	0.13
			Girls	10.1	2.47	
		Locale	Rural	11.13	1.83	2.07*
			Urban	9.83	2.67	
		Management Of School	Government	10.88	2.45	1.90
			Private	9.70	2.30	
2.	Understanding	Sex	Boys	15.64	5.9	0.65
			Girls	16.56	5.07	
		Locale	Rural	15.71	5.34	0.49

contd...

Sl. No.	*Instructional Objectives*	*Variables*	*Sub Samples*	*Mean*	*Standard Deviation*	*Critical Ratio*
			Urban	16.42	5.57	
		Management	Government	16.35	5.35	1.13
		Of School	Private	15.36	5.53	
3.	Application	Sex	Boys	5.79	1.95	0.54
			Girls	5.00	1.67	
		Locale	Rural	5.21	1.91	0.54
			Urban	5.47	1.03	
		Management	Government	5.48	3.2	0.55
		Of School	Private	5.22	3.64	
4.	Skill	Sex	Boys	4.46	1.62	1.84
			Girls	3.72	1.51	
		Locale	Rural	4.79	1.67	3.08**
			Urban	3.58	1.36	
		Management	Government	4.09	1.79	0.13
		Of School	Private	4.04	1.91	

Details from Table 16 revealed that there was no difference between the sub samples compared with respect to immediate post test achievement scores for the categories Understanding and Application. This finding implied that when students were taught using Discovery learning the sub samples viz., Boys and Girls; students belonging to Rural and urban schools and students belonging to Government and Private schools exhibited similar performance with regard to understanding of the facts and concepts of adaptations, interpreting verbal material and making predictions regarding the structural and functional adaptations displayed in living organisms. Students of rural schools displayed superior performance in defining, describing the process of adaptation, in identifying feeding habit of birds and in making illustrations of birds based on data provided than students of urban schools.

Details from Table 17 revealed that there was significant difference between the Treatment groups LMG and MMG with respect to realization of instructional objectives belonging to the categories—Knowledge, Understanding, Application and Skill. The differences were in favor of Memorization strategy group. It can be concluded that using memorization techniques enhances the knowledge of students concerning the term Planaria, understanding of the structural peculiarities of Planaria, applying the knowledge of terms obtained to interpret and define associated scientific terms in other contexts using memorization strategies. Research studies conducted earlier have revealed that various Memorization strategies enhances the knowledge of students (Weinstein, 1982). These results are also in consistent with previous research findings (Doctorow et al 1978, Gregg, 1987; Levin et al, 1988; Meyer et al 1980; Weinstein; 1982).

TABLE 17

***t*-test Between Means of Immediate Post Test Scores of MMG and LMG - Realization of Instructional Objective (Total Sample)**

Instructional Objective	*Mean (M)*		*Standard Deviation (S.D)*		*Critical Ratio (CR)*
	DLM	*LM*	*DLM*	*LM*	
Knowledge	9.0	9.94	2.0	2.10	2.4*
Understanding	16.2	11.4	3.9	4.53	6.2**
Application	7.3	5.4	2.2	3.11	3.8**
Skill	4.4	2.8	1.3	1.4	6.6**

** Significant at .01 level

Details from Table 18 revealed that there was no difference between the sub samples compared with respect to immediate post test achievement scores for the categories Understanding and Skill. This finding implies that the sub samples compared viz., Boys and Girls; students belonging to Rural and urban schools and students belonging to Government and Private schools exhibited similar performances in understanding of the facts related to the nature of organisms included in the

TABLE 18

Realization of Instructional Objectives When Students are Taught Through Memorization Strategies

Sl. No.	*Instructional Objectives*	*Variables*	*Sub Samples*	*Mean*	*Standard Deviation*	*Critical Ratio*
1.	Knowledge	Sex	Boys	9.4	2.11	1.62
			Girls	8.6	1.71	
		Locale	Rural	9.67	1.83	2.23*
			Urban	8.56	1.92	
		Management	Government	9.48	1.84	2.2*
		Of School	Private	8.41	1.95	
2.	Understanding	Sex	Boys	16.47	4.17	0.69
			Girls	15..93	3.71	(NS)
		Locale	Rural	15.92	3.49	0.45
			Urban	16.39	4.22	(NS)
		Management	Government	16.18	1.84	0.04
		Of School	Private	16.22	1.95	(NS)
3.	Application	Sex	Boys	7.53	2.62	0.88
			Girls	6.97	1.77	(NS)
		Locale	Rural	8.38	1.69	3.46**
			Urban	6.5	2.26	
		Management	Government	7.85	2.03	2.38*
		Of School	Private	6.52	2.3	
4.	Skill	Sex	Boys	4.27	1.28	0.70
			Girls	4.47	1.25	(NS)
		Locale	Rural	4.33	1.31	0.16
			Urban	4.39	1.25	(NS)
		Management	Government	4.55	1.28	1.22
		Of School	Private	4.15	1.23	(NS)

**Significant at .01 level NS- Not significant
* Significant at .05 level.

phylum Platyhelminthes, anatomical and physiological peculiarities and life habits of Planaria when memorization techniques were used for teaching/learning Biology. However, students of Rural schools and Government schools were found to be superior to their counterparts in indicating familiarity and recall of the terms related to Plan aria and in applying the knowledge of terms obtained to interpret and define associated scientific terms in other contexts when memorization strategies were implemented in the classroom. More follow-up studies require to be done to cite reasons for superior performance of these sub samples.

TABLE 19

t-test between Means of Immediate Post Test Scores of CBG and LMG – Realization of Instructional Objective (Total Sample)

Instructional Objective	*Mean (M)*		*Standard Deviation (S.D)*		*Critical Ratio (CR)*
	DLM	*LM*	*DLM*	*LM*	
Knowledge	9.47	10.63	4.2	1.7	1.4 (NS)
Understanding	14.5	9.1	4.23	1.69	6.9**
Application	8.2	4.0	2.83	2.4	7.0**
Skill	5.1	3.3	1.3	0.95	6.7**

** Significant at .01 level

Details from Table 19 revealed that three was significant difference between Lecture method and Computer based Method with respect to realization of instructional objectives belonging to the categories Understanding, Application and Skill. The differences were in favor of Computer based Method. It can be concluded that using Computer as a learning tool enhances the realization of instructional objectives belonging to the categories Understanding, Application and Skill. The results revealed that learning the details of cell structure and function through computers contributed to developing better understanding of the cellular processes, structure-function relationship of cell organelles and in applying the knowledge obtained in day to day life. It also enhanced skills of observation, presenting details observed in diagrams and labeling parts drawn. These results are in tune with Research findings reported on similar contexts earlier (Vaidyan, 1989; Jegede et al (1991); Aguire et al (1997); Defrieze 1997; Chadwick and Hutton (1997).

TABLE 20

Realization of Instructional Objectives When Students are Taught Through Computer Based Method: *Comparison of Various Subsampless*

Sl. No.	*Instructional Objectives*	*Variables*	*Sub Samples*	*Mean*	*Standard Deviation*	*Critical Ratio*
1.	Knowledge	Sex	Boys	8.4	2.59	2.16*
			Girls	10.6	2.99	
		Management	Government	9	2.83	1.5
		Of School	Private	10.8	2.53	(NS)
2	Understanding	Sex	Boys	14.04	4.88	0.54
			Girls	14.88	3.46	(NS)
		Management	Government	15.09	4.64	0.67
		Of School	Private	13.83	3.69	(NS)
3	Application	Sex	Boys	8.07	2.28	0.43
			Girls	8.4	1.99	(NS)
		Management	Government	8.0	2.31	0.98
		Of School	Private	8.01	2.38	(NS)
4	Skill	Sex	Boys	4.93	1.03	0.63
			Girls	5.20	1.26	(NS)
		Management	Government	4.7	1.06	1.53
		Of School	Private	5.50	1.27	(NS)

Details from Table 20 revealed that there was significant difference between Boys and girls with regard to realization of instructional objectives belonging to category Knowledge. Girls were found to be superior to Boys in recalling terms related to cell when taught through computer based instruction. Results revealed that computer based method was equally beneficial for boys and girls, students of government and private schools in realizing the instructional objectives belonging to categories Understanding, Application and Skill. This finding implies that use of Computer as a learning tool was found to enhance realization of instructional objectives belonging to categories Understanding, Application and Skill.

PART II

5.5.0 Comparative Cffectiveness of DLM, MM and CBM in Attaining Select Educational Outcomes –Ratings of Experts

This section is intended to give details regarding the comparative effectiveness of DLM, MM and CBM in attaining select Educational outcomes based on ratings of Experts. The necessary data were collected by administering a Judgment schedule to Experts (N=10). For convenience the statements (The same statements were included in the Judgment Schedule for teachers) in the Judgment Schedule were classified under the following dimensions.

1. Cognitive
2. Affective
3. Process Skills
4. Social

The details of the ratings of experts (in Percentages) is given in Tables 21-24.

5.5.1 Effect of Instructional Method on Attaining Educational Outcomes Included Under Cognitive Dimension

The ratings given by Experts on the three instructional models in attaining educational outcomes listed under cognitive dimension is given in Table 21.

TABLE 21

Ratings of Experts on Comparative Effectiveness of DLM, MM and CBM: Cognitive

Sl No.	*Educational Outcome*	*Response Percentage*								
		DLM			*MM*			*CBM*		
		GE	*SE*	*NA*	*GE*	*SE*	*NA*	*GE*	*SE*	*NA*
1.	Helps to retain learnt facts	100	0	0	100	0	0	0	100	0
2.	Promote easier transfer of learning	100	0	0	10	90	0	90	10	0
3.	Applies learnt facts in new situations	100	0	0	10	80	10	0	90	10
4.	Helps to predict Biological phenomenon	90	10	0	0	25	75	10	80	10
5.	Derives generalizations from Environmental situations	80	20	0	20	30	50	0	70	30
6.	Develops general principles about Nature and Natural Phenomenon	80	20	0	0	0	100	10	75	15
7.	Establishes structure-function relationship	90	10	0	0	10	90	10	80	10

It is evident from Table 21 that cent percent of Experts recorded that DLM was effective to A GREAT EXTENT in helping retention, applying learnt facts and transfer of learning. Majority of the experts agreed that Discovery learning was effective to a GREAT EXTENT in attaining the other listed Cognitive Outcomes. Regarding the effectiveness of MM, cent percent of Experts recorded that MM is effective to A **Great Extent** in *Retaining learnt facts.* Cent percent of Experts recorded that CBM is effective to A Great Extent *in promoting easier transfer of learning.* Majority of Teachers recorded that

CBM was effective to SOME EXTENT in attaining the following Educational Outcomes: *in retaining learnt facts (90%); Applying learnt facts in new situations (90%); Predicting Biological phenomenon (80%);. Establishing structure –function relationship (90%).*

5.5.2 Effect of Instructional Method on Attaining Educational Outcomes Included Under Affective Dimension

The ratings given by Experts on the three instructional models in attaining educational outcomes listed under affective dimension is given in Table 22.

TABLE 22

Ratings of Experts on Comparative Effectiveness of DLM, MM and CBM: Affective

Sl No.	*Educational Outcome*	*Response Percentage*								
		DLM			*MM*			*CBM*		
		GE	*SE*	*NA*	*GE*	*SE*	*NA*	*GE*	*SE*	*NA*
1.	Develops positive attitude towards Biology	100	0	0	10	90	0	80	20	0
2.	Develops interest in Science related activities	100	0	0	20	80	0	90	10	0
3.	Appreciates diversity of Nature	100	0	0	20	80	0	10	90	0
4.	Develops curiosity to know more about Biological phenomenon	100	0	0	20	80	0	80	20	0
5.	Develops interest in issues having Global implications	10	90	0	20	80	0	70	30	0
6.	Develops interest in Nature study	100	0	0	20	80	0	30	70	0
7.	Develops interest in Life History and contributions of scientists	0	100	0	10	90	0	20	80	0

It is evident from Table 22 that cent percent of Experts recorded that DLM and majority of experts recorded that MM was effective to A Great Extent in attaining most of the Educational Outcomes included under the affective dimension. Majority of experts recorded that CBM was effective to A Great Extent in attaining the following Educational Outcomes: *Developing positive attitude towards Biology (80%); Developing interest in Science related activities (90%); Developing curiosity to know more about Biological phenomenon (80%)*

5.5.3 Effect of Instructional Method on Attaining Educational Outcomes Included Under Process Skills Dimension

TABLE 23

Ratings of Experts on Comparative Effectiveness of DLM, MM and CBM: Process Skills

Sl No.	*Educational Outcome*	*Response Percentage*								
		DLM			*MM*			*CBM*		
		GE	*SE*	*NA*	*GE*	*SE*	*NA*	*GE*	*SE*	*NA*
1.	*Observation*	100	0	0	20	80	0	20	80	0
2.	*Classification*	100	0	0	30	70	0	10	80	10
3.	*Formulating hypothesis*	100	0	0	0	0	100	40	60	0
4.	*Testing Hypothesis*	100	0	0	0	0	100	30	70	0
5.	*Analyzing data and Interpreting data*	10	90	0	0	0	100	20	80	0
6.	*Discovering Relationship*	100	0	0	0	90	10	20	80	0
7.	*Problem solving*	0	100	0	0	90	10	20	80	0

The ratings given by Experts on the three instructional models in attaining educational outcomes listed under Process Skills dimension is given in Table 23.

Cent percent of Experts recorded that DLM was effective to A Great Extent in Developing Skills in *Observation, Classification, Formulating hypothesis, Testing Hypothesis, Analysing and Interpreting data, Discovering Relationship and Problem solving.*

Cent per cent of Experts recorded that MM was NOT AT ALL effective *in developing skills in Formulating hypothesis, Testing Hypothesis, Analyzing and Interpreting data.* Analysis of data also revealed that Majority of Experts reported that CBM was effective **to some extent** *in developing various process skills related to Biology.*

5.5.4 Effect of Instructional Method on Attaining Educational Outcomes Included Under Social Dimension

The ratings given by Experts on the three instructional models in attaining educational outcomes listed under Social dimension is given in Table 24.

It is evident from Table 24 that cent percent of Experts recorded that DLM was effective to A GREAT EXTENT in attaining all the Educational Outcomes listed under Social dimension: Majority of Experts (Table 24) reported that MM was effective to a GREAT EXTENT in attaining the following Educational Outcomes listed under Social dimension: *Promoting Teacher-student interaction (90%), Providing Excellent situations for discussions (90%), Providing opportunities for Pupil Participation (80%,); Stimulating sharing of ideas among students (90%).* Regarding the effectiveness of CBM, majority of Experts reported that CBM was effective to a GREAT EXTENT *in Providing opportunities for Pupil Participation (80%) and Stimulating sharing of ideas among students.*

TABLE 24

Ratings of Experts on Comparative Effectiveness of DLM, MM and CBM: Social

Sl No.	*Educational Outcome*	*DLM*			*MM*			*CBM*		
		GE	*SE*	*NA*	*GE*	*SE*	*NA*	*GE*	*SE*	*NA*
1.	*Promotes Teacher-student interaction*	100	0	0	90	10	0	20	20	60
2.	*Provides Excellent situations for discussions*	100	0	0	90	10	0	0	20	80
3.	*Promotes situations for Group activities*	100	0	0	80	20	0	0	80	20
4.	*Provides opportunities for Pupil Participation*	100	0	0	90	10	0	0	80	20
5.	*Develops spirit of team work among students*	*100*	*0*	*0*	*0*	*100*	*0*	*0*	*80*	*20*
6.	*Stimulates sharing of ideas among students*	100	0	0	90	10	0	20	80	0
7.	*Promotes sense of belonging to a group*	*100*	*0*	*0*	*90*	*10*	*0*	*75*	*25*	*0*

5.6.0 Ratings of Teachers on the Comparative Effectiveness of DLM, MM, CBM and LM in Attaining Select Educational Outcomes

This section is intended to give details regarding the comparative effectiveness of Discovery Learning Model (DLM), Memory Model (MM), Computer based Model (CBM) with that of Lecture Method (LM) in attaining select Educational outcomes based on ratings of Teachers. The necessary data were collected by administering a Judgment schedule to Teachers (N=90). For convenience the statements included in the Judgment Schedule were classified under the following dimensions.

1. Cognitive

2. Affective
3. Process Skills
4. Social Interaction

The ratings of Teachers were recorded against a five point scale Very High (VH), High (H), Medium (M), Low (L) and Very Low (VL) a (✓) mark in the appropriate column. The tests of significance for difference between means of the developed models DLM, MM and CBM and LM were calculated for each outcome in the schedule. The details are given in Tables 25 -27.

5.6.1 Effectiveness of DLM and LM in Attaining Select Educational Outcomes

Details regarding the tests of significance for difference between means of ratings of teachers about the effectiveness of DLM and LM in attaining select Educational Outcomes is given in Table 25.

TABLE 25

***t-test* Between Means of DLM and LM for Select Educational Outcome**

Educational outcomes	*Mean*		*Standard Deviation*		*Critical ratio*
	DLM	*LM*	*DLM*	*LM*	
Cognitive	31.69	28.9	2.25	3.02	4.21*
Affective	32.90	15.2	1.75	4.58	19.96*
Process Skills	27.67	11.7	4.88	1.76	18.35*
Social Interaction	20.77	11.53	2.01	2.03	16.29*

* Significant at .01 level

There was significant difference between DLM and LM with respect to attaining Educational Outcomes under the following dimensions, Cognitive CR=4.21;p<.01; Affective (CR =19.96;P<.01); Process Skills (CR = 18.35; P<.01). Social Interaction (CR = 16.29; P<.01). The differences were in favour of DLM for all the dimensions considered. From the results it can be implied that DLM is superior to LM in terms of attaining Educational Outcomes belonging to the Cognitive, Affective, Process Skills and Social Interaction. These findings have been supported by studies conducted earlier by Driver (1989), Bruner (1965), Wittrock (1966) (Worthen, 1968; Tamir and Goldminz, 1974; Selim and Shrigley (1983).

5.6.2 Effectiveness of MM and LM in Attaining Select Educational Outcomes

Details regarding the tests of significance for difference between means of ratings of teachers about the effectiveness of MM and LM in attaining select Educational Outcomes is given in Table 26.

TABLE 26

***t*-test Between Mean Scores of MM and LM for Select Educational Outcomes**

Educational outcomes	*Mean* DLM	*LM*	*Standard Deviation* DLM	*LM*	*Critical ratio*
Cognitive	31.03	28.89	2.85	3.02	2.83**
Affective	28.04	15.20	2.74	4.58	13.18**
Process Skills	16.07	11.17	3.13	1.76	7.47
Social Interaction	20.83	11.5	5.41	2.01	8.82**

*Significant at .01 Level.

There is significant difference between MM and LM with respect to attaining Educational Outcomes under the following dimensions, Cognitive (CR = 2.83; P<.01); Affective (*CR* = 13.18; P<.01). Process Skills (*CR* = 7.47; P<.01) and Social Interaction (C*R* = 8.82; P<.01). The differences were in favour of MM for all the dimensions considered. From the results it can be implied that MM was superior to LM in terms of attaining Educational Outcomes belonging to the Cognitive, Affective, Process Skills and Social Interaction.

5.6.3 Effectiveness of CBM and LM in Attaining Select Educational Outcomes

Details regarding the tests of significance for difference between means of ratings of teachers about the effectiveness of CBM and LM in attaining select Educational Outcomes is given in Table 27.

TABLE 27

***t*-test Between Mean Scores of CBM and LM for Select Educational Outcome**

Educational outcomes	*Mean* DLM	LM	*Standard Deviation* DLM	LM	*Critical ratio*
Cognitive	29.26	28.89	2.45	3.02	0.53
Affective	18.99	15.20	2.96	4.58	3.81**
Process Skills	22.43	11.17	4.67	1.76	12.37**
Social Interaction	10.47	11.53	3.59	2.01	1.42

**Significant at .01 Level.

Details in Table 27 revealed that there was significant difference between CBM and LM in attaining Educational Outcomes under the following dimensions, Affective *CR* = 13.18; P<.01 and Process Skills CR = 7.47; P<.01. The difference was in favour of CBM for these dimensions. From the results it can be concluded that CBM was superior to LM in terms of attaining Educational Outcomes included under the dimensions Affective and Process Skills. This has been substantiated by studies conducted earlier (Defreize, 1997; Breithaupt, 1997; Blount, 1997; Collis, 1988).

PART III

Suitability of Models: Discovery Learning Model (DLM), Memory Model (MM) and Computer based Model (CBM)

This section deals with the analysis of ratings of teachers (N=90) regarding the suitability of the developed models viz., DLM, MM and CBM with regard to availability, extent of practice, and feasibility with regard to curricular aspects for teaching Biology at secondary level. The necessary data were collected by administering a questionnaire to Secondary School Teachers. The percentages of all the responses for each item were calculated. The details are given under appropriate heads.

5.7.1 Availability of Learning Resources and Extent of Practice for Using the Models

Details regarding the Availability of learning resources and extent of practice for using the models viz., Discovery learning model, Memory model and computer based model are given in Table 28.

TABLE– 28

Availability of Learning Resources and Extent of Practice for Using the Models

Outcome factors	*DLM (Rating in %)*			*MM (Rating in %)*			*CBM (Ratings in %)*		
	GE	*SE*	*NA*	*GE*	*SE*	*NA*	*GE*	*SE*	*NA*
1. Availability of Resources For Teaching Biology using the Models	20	80	0	63	27	10	0	13	87
2. Extent of practice of the developed models	10	14	76	24	43	33	0	0	100

GE-Great Extent; SE-Some Extent; NA-Not At All

80 % of teachers reported that Resources are available for learning/teaching Biology using DLM only to Some extent, whereas 63 % percent of the teachers reported that resources were available for using memorization strategies

to a GREAT EXTENT. Majority of teachers (87%) reported that Learning resources are NOT AT ALL available to teach Biology using Computer Based Method.

Lack of learning resources may be the reason for the dismally low extent of practice of the Discovery learning method (10%) and none of the teachers resorted to computer based method. However only 43% of teachers were using memorization strategies.

5.7.2 Suitability of Developed Models

Details regarding the suitability for using the models viz., Discovery learning model, Memory model and computer based model based on ratings given by teachers are given in Table 29.

TABLE 29

Ratings of Teachers Regarding the Suitability of Developed Models

Outcome factors	*DLM (Rating in %)*			*MM (Rating in %)*			*CBM (Ratings in %)*		
	GE	*SE*	*NA*	*GE*	*SE*	*NA*	*GE*	*SE*	*NA*
Syllabus	100	0	0	33	67	0	0	100	0
Time-Table	0	100	0	33	67	0	0	100	0
Examination	0	100	0	100	0	0	0	100	0
Teacher Training	100	0	0	100	0	0	10	67	23

Cent percent of teachers reported that implementing Discovery learning method and computer based method were conducive to existing curricular aspects of Time table and conduct of examinations to SOME EXTENT. Cent percent of teachers reported that awareness of memorization strategies were helpful for students in performance in examinations and the Teacher education programme was conducive to make student trainees competent in use of memorization techniques. With regard to computer based instruction only 67% of teachers reported existing teacher education programme is suitable in transferring skills for implementing computer assisted instruction in the classroom. This result emphasizes the need to restructure the Teacher Education Curriculum so as to equip teachers in imparting computer based instruction to students.

5.7.3 Practical Difficulties Encountered by Teachers While Using DLM, MM and CBM

This section is intended to give details regarding the practical difficulties recorded by teachers while using DLM, MM and CBM (for teaching Biology). Kendell's co-efficient of concordance was used for calculating the practical difficulties likely to be encountered by teachers while practicing the developed models viz., DLM, MM and CBM. The details are given in Tables 30-32.

(i) Practical Difficulties Encountered by Teachers While Using DLM

Details regarding the practical difficulties likely to be encountered by teachers while using DLM is given in Table 30.

It is evident from Table 30 that the co-efficient of concordance is significant at .01 level (W = 168; P<.01). The result reveals that there is agreement among the teachers with regard to assigning ranks to the listed difficulties. The sum of ranks is least (S= 6) for the difficulties **lack of library facilities** and **Overloaded Syllabus** hence it can be concluded that teachers feel that lack of library resources and the lack of time for completing the syllabus are major constraints in using Discovery Learning Method. The following difficulties were also identified: Rigid Time Table (S=11), lack of suitable evaluation measures (S=15), lack of Co-operation of authorities (S=16), Over crowded classrooms (S=26), lack of training for teachers (S=31) and lack of time for preparation of lesson (S=114). The result pointed out the need for equipping the library with adequate reference materials.

TABLE 30

Co-efficient of Concordance for Practical Difficulties: DLM

Sl. No.	*Difficulties faced by Teachers*	*Sum of ranks*	*W*
1.	Rigid Time Table	10	
2.	Over crowded Syllabus	16	
1.	Overcrowded classrooms	26	
2.	Rigid Time Table	11	
3.	Lack of Library Facilities	6	
4.	Overloaded Syllabus	6	
5.	Lack of co-operation of authorities	114	168
6.	Lack of time for preparation of lesson	16	
7.	Lack of suitable evaluation Measures	15	
8.	Lack of training for teachers	31	

(ii) Practical Difficulties Encountered by Teachers While Using MM

Details regarding the practical difficulties likely to be encountered by teachers while using MM is given in Table 31.

It is evident from Table 31 that the co-efficient of concordance calculated is significant at .01 level (W = 28.14; P<.01). The result reveals that there is agreement among the teachers with regard to assigning ranks to the listed difficulties.

The sum of ranks is least for the difficulty **Rigid time-**table (S=10). The following difficulties were also identified while using Memory Method: Overcrowded syllabus (S=16), inadequate Knowledge about Innovative teaching methods (S=21), lack of time for planning lesson plans (S=28). It can be concluded that teachers feel that rigidity of the time-table is a major constraint for practicing Memory Method. This result emphasized the need to make the time table more flexible.

TABLE 31

Co-efficient of Concordance for Practical Difficulties: MM

Sl. No.	*Difficulties faced by Teachers*	*Sum of ranks*	*W*
1.	Rigid Time Table	10	
2.	Over crowded Syllabus	16	
3.	Inadequate Knowledge about innovative teaching methods	21	**28.14**
4.	Lack of time required for planning and preparing lesson plans	28	
5.	No Library facilities	30	
6.	Lack of training to use innovative teaching methods	30	
7.	Over crowded Classrooms	35	
8.	Lack of Co-operation among authorities	64	

(iii) Practical Difficulties Encountered by Teachers While Using CBM

Details regarding the practical difficulties likely to be encountered by teachers while using CBM is given in Table 32.

It is evident from Table 32 that the co-efficient of concordance calculated is significant at .01 level (W = 348; P<.01). The result revealed that there is agreement among the teachers with regard to assigning ranks to the listed difficulties. The sum of ranks is least (S=6) for the difficulty Rigid time-table and hence it can be concluded that teachers feel that rigidity of the time-table is a major constraint to implementing Computer-based Method.

TABLE 32

Co-efficient of Concordance for Practical Difficulties: CBM

Sl. No.	*Difficulties faced by Teachers*	*Sum of ranks*	*W*
1.	Lack of Library Facilities	84	
2.	Rigid Time Table	6	
3.	Inadequate knowledge about innovative teaching methods.	72	348*
4.	Difficulty in Maintaining discipline	36	
5.	Lack of Computers	39	
6.	Lack of time required for planning and preparing lesson plans	42	
7.	Overloaded syllabus	54	

** Significant at .01 level

5.7.4 Suggestions Given by Teachers for Successful Implementation of Developed Models

Details regarding the suggestions given by teachers for successful implementation of Discovery Learning Method, Memory Method and Computer based Method is given in Table 33

TABLE 33

Suggestions Given by Teachers with Respect to Developed Models

Model	*Suggestions given by Teachers*	*No.*	*%*
DLM	1. The time table should be made flexible so as to incorporate discovery learning	18	20
	2. Teachers should be given training	24	26
	3. Suitable content should be included in the Syllabus.	18	20
MM	1. The School should encourage and give emphasis to innovative teaching strategies	21	23

contd...

Model	Suggestions given by Teachers	No.	%
	2. Text book content should be restructured for adopting computer based approach	36	40
CBM	1. Curriculum should incorporate Computer Instruction at secondary level	32	36
	2. Overcrowding in Classrooms should be Avoided	41	46
	3. Facilities should be built for computer Instruction.	45	50

It is evident from Table 33 that as regards the successful implementation of Discovery Learning Model in the classroom 20% of teachers suggested that the Time Table should be made flexible so as to incorporate Discovery Learning.

With regard to the implementation of Memory Model the following suggestions were made: *Teachers should be given training in Memory Models* (26%) and *Teacher's Handbook should contain guidelines for use of memorization techniques* (20%).

As regards the Computer-based Model it was suggested that facilities should be provided for offering computer-assisted instruction for various subjects (50%). It was followed by *Teacher- pupil ratio should be reduced* (46%), *Text Book should be supported with computer software program* (40%) and *curriculum should incorporate Computer Instruction at Secondary level* (36%).

6

Findings, Discussion of Results, Recommendations and Implications of the Study

This study was planned to know the effectiveness of models based on Discovery learning, Memorizations strategies and computer based instruction in learning select topics in Biology. The achievement scores (Pre-test, immediate post-test, delayed memory test and Extent of Forgetting) of the experimental groups ((Discovery learning Group (DLG), Memory Method Group (MMG) and Computer based group (CBG)) was compared with the control group (Lecture method group (LMG). In the previous chapter the data were analyzed and interpreted employing various statistical techniques. In this chapter the findings and their discussions, educational implications and recommendations for further research are presented.

Effect of Instructional Methods on Achievement—Total Sample

To test the effectiveness of the developed models viz., Discovery Learning Model (DLM), Memory Model (MM) and Computer based Model (CBM) the mean pre test achievement scores of the experimental groups was compared with the lecture method group in each casé. Results showed no significant difference between means of the experimental groups and control group with regard to pre test achievement. This implied that the groups were similar before the experimental teaching.

To test the effectiveness of the models with regard to achievement in Biology for immediate post test achievement, Delayed Memory achievement and Extent of Forgetting the scores obtained for Experimental groups was compared with those of the control group. The tests of significance for difference between means was used to interpret results. Results indicated significant difference between Experimental groups and control group for all the three achievement scores. Immediate post test achievement, Delayed memory achievement and Extent of Forgetting. The differences were in favor of the Experimental group in each case. It can be concluded therefore that all the three models were superior to Lecture method for achievement in Biology. The developed models were also effective in enhancing retention as was evidenced by the significantly lower Extent of Forgetting scores in each case.

Effect of Instructional Methods on Achievement.-Sub Samples

The retention power of girls was found to be better than boys when taught using Discovery learning. The achievement in Biology was not influenced by the locale of the school when taught through Discovery Learning Method as Students of Rural and Urban schools did not exhibit any significant difference with respect to Immediate post test achievement, Delayed memory achievement and Extent of Forgetting. Students of Private schools were found to have better retention than students of Government schools when taught using Discovery learning.

Teaching through Memorization strategies was found to enhance the immediate post test achievement, Delayed memory achievement and retention power among students. The Post test achievement of students of rural and Government schools were found to enhance when memorization strategies were used. The memorization strategies used were found to be effective more for Boys, students of Rural and government schools more than their counterparts. This implied use of memorization strategies for boys, students of rural and government schools. This finding highlights the need for teachers to resort to dynamic methods of teaching and to take into account the nature of the school and students while teaching Biology.

Teaching through Computer based method enhanced the immediate post test achievement, Delayed memory achievement and retention power among students. Computer based learning environments was found to be more effective for girls and students of Government schools. The particular result may be due to the fact that it is possible that girls and students of government schools were likely to have less access to computers. This highlights the need to introduce computers as learning tools for girls and students of government schools.

Effect of Instructional Method on Realization of Objectives

Discovery Learning method was superior to Lecture method in the realization of instructional objectives belonging to the categories Knowledge, Understanding, Application and Skill. Boys and Girls; students belonging to Rural and urban schools and students belonging to Government and Private schools exhibited similar performance with regard to understanding of the facts and concepts of adaptations and making predictions regarding the structural and functional adaptations displayed in living organisms when the select topic was taught using Discovery learning method. Students of rural schools displayed superior performance in defining, describing the process of adaptation, in identifying feeding habit of birds and in making illustrations of birds based on data provided than students of urban schools. This finding highlights the need for teachers to resort to dynamic methods of teaching and adopt appropriate methods to suit the leaning abilities, innate capabilities, prior knowledge and attitude of students.

Teaching through memorization techniques enhanced the realization of all the instructional objectives belonging to the categories Knowledge, Understanding, Application and Skill. There was no difference between the sub samples compared with respect to immediate post test achievement scores for the categories Understanding and Skill. Using memorization techniques enhanced the knowledge of students concerning the term Planaria, understanding of the structural peculiarities of Planaria, applying the knowledge of terms obtained to interpret and define associated scientific terms in other contexts using memorization strategies. More follow-up studies require to be done to make further deductions regarding the effect of memorization.

There was significant difference between Lecture method and Computer based Method with respect to realization of instructional objectives belonging to the categories Understanding, Application and Skill. The differences were in favour of Computer based Method. It can be concluded that using Computer as a learning tool enhances the realization of instructional objectives belonging to the categories Understanding, Application and Skill there was no difference between the sub samples compared with respect to immediate post test achievement scores for the categories Understanding and Skill. Learning the details of cell structure and function through computers contributed to developing better understanding of the cellular processes, structure-function relationship of cell organelles and in applying the knowledge obtained in day to day life. It also enhanced skills of observation, drawing and identifying and reproducing illustrations of cell and cell organelles.

Effect of Instructional Method in Attaining Educational Outcomes-Ratings of Experts

For Discovery learning most of the listed cognitive outcomes were rated as being effective to a great extent by all the experts. Memorization strategies were rated as being effective to a great extent by cent per cent of the experts for helping in retention of learnt facts. Nevertheless, the experts did not find favour with memorization techniques as being effective in attaining the other listed cognitive outcomes viz., developing principles of natural phenomenon. The computer based method was rated as being effective to some extent in attaining cognitive outcomes.

All the experts agreed that Discovery learning was effective to a great extent in attaining affective outcomes. Majority of experts agreed that memorization strategies was effective to some extent in attaining affective outcomes. Majority of experts rated computer based method as being effective to a great extent in attaining some of the listed affective outcomes viz., developing positive attitude, interest and curiosity.

All the experts agreed that Discovery learning was effective to a great extent in attaining Process Skills outcomes. All the experts rated memorization strategies as being Not at all effective in developing skills in formulating hypothesis, testing hypothesis and analysis and interpretation of data. Majority of experts rated computer based method as being effective to some extent in attaining Process Skills outcomes.

All the experts agreed that Discovery learning was effective to a great extent in attaining Social outcomes. Majority of experts agreed that memorization strategies was effective to a great extent in attaining social outcomes viz., providing scope for pupil participation, sharing ideas, group activities and collaborative learning. Majority of experts rated computer based method as being effective to a some extent in attaining some of the listed social outcomes viz., providing scope for pupil participation, sharing ideas, group activities and collaborative learning.

Effect of Instructional Method in Attaining Educational Outcomes—Ratings of Teachers

The teachers rated the developed models Discovery learning method and memory method superior to Lecture method for attaining Educational outcomes included under the dimensions—Cognitive, Affective, Process skills and social. The ratings given by teachers has been further supported by the comparison of achievement scores of Experimental (Discovery learning Group and Memory method group) for the categories—Knowledge, Understanding, Application and Skill and the ratings of experts. The teachers rated the computer based method as being superior to lecture method in attaining Educational outcomes included under the dimensions Affective and Process Skills. Comparison of achievement scores of computer based group had revealed the superiority of the experimental group over the control group in realizing instructional objectives included under the categories Understanding, Application and Skill. Positive results of computer based method in attaining cognitive outcomes (Understanding and Application) have been obtained in contrary to negative ratings' given by experts and teachers. This may be due to the nature of the software, interesting introduction, novel facts, interactive presentation of the topic, provision for immediate feedback.

Suitability of Existing Curricular Aspects for Successful Implementation of Models

Majority of the teachers rated that resources were available for successful implementation of Discovery learning in the classroom only to Some Extent, whereas resources were available to a great extent for using memorization techniques, but resources were Not at All available for implementing computer based instruction. This may be cited as a reason for majority of teachers Not at all practicing Discovery learning in the classroom and memorization strategies practiced only by a minority of teachers (33%) and None of the teachers were practicing Computer based instruction.

All the teachers rated that curricular aspects of Syllabus and Teacher education programme were conducive to a great extent for implementing Discovery learning, All the teachers rated that memorization strategies were suitable to a great extent with respect to prevailing system of examinations and the teacher education programme whereas all the teachers rated that computer based instruction was suitable to some extent with respect to prevailing content and scope of syllabus, structure of Time table and conduct of examinations.

Practical Difficulties Likely to be Encountered by Teachers

There was consistency in ranks assigned to the enlisted difficulties likely to be encountered by teachers while using the developed models. Teachers feel that lack of library resources and the lack of time for completing the syllabus are major constraints in using Discovery Learning Method. The result pointed out the need for equipping the library with adequate reference materials. It was revealed that teachers feel that rigidity of the time-table is a major constraint for practicing Memory Method and computer based instruction. This result emphasized the need to make the time table more flexible.

Suggestions Given by Teachers

Flexibility in the Time table was suggested by teachers for successful implementation of Discovery Learning Model. Imparting training in use of memorization strategies and the

Teacher's handbook should give suitable guidelines when, how and where these memorization techniques can be employed was suggested for successful implementation of memory method. For effective computer based instruction it was suggested that the classroom strength should be reduced, Text Book should be supported with computer software program and curriculum should incorporate Computer Instruction at Secondary level.

Discussion

The findings implied that the developed models when implemented in the classroom was superior to the lecture method in recording achievement in Biology while teaching the particular topics. These instructional strategies were also found to enhance the achievement in Biology.

Discovery learning has been found to enhance achievement in research studies conducted earlier (Worthen, 1968; Selim and Shrigley (1983); Shymansky, (1983), Prema (1995), Beena (1997).

Memorizations strategies were found to be superior to lecture method and was also found to enhance achievement in Biology. Studies have reported that memorization strategies can influence academic performance by improving retention and better retrieval of content learnt (Arkes et al, 1976; Rickards and August, 1975; Howe, 1970; Levin et al, 1982).

With respect to realization of instructional objectives the developed models were found to be superior to lecture method in realizing the instructional objectives belonging to the categories Knowledge, Understanding, Application and Skill. Research studies conducted earlier have revealed that various Memorization strategies enhances the knowledge of students (Weinstein, 1982). These results are also in consistent with previous research findings (Doctorow et al 1978, Gregg, 1987; Levin et al, 1988; Meyer et al 1980; Weinstein; 1982).

Computer as a learning tool was found to enrich the learning environment, enhance the learning process, make education more widely available and produce cost-effective solution to the dissemination of knowledge (Chein, 1997, Crawford, 1997; McClure, 1996; Reinking, 1988; Rosner, 1997; Vaidyan, 1989,). This impact is not consistent across different subjects and various age groups(Johnson et al, 1994).

It was found to improve student achievement, thinking, skills,motivation, social skills, meta-cognition and communication (Hildinger, 1997; Lakshmi, 2000; Joshi and Mahapatra, 1997; Machado, 1997; Seguin, 1995).

The ratings given by experts for the developed models revealed the superiority of Discovery learning being a process approach in attaining Cognitive, affective and process skills outcomes. Classroom approaches of Discovery learning and memorization strategies in enhanced social skills and provided opportunities for sharing and communicating ideas.

Recommendations

The developed models were effective in enhancing achievement in Biology hence attempts should be taken to encourage teachers to make use of these learning strategies in the classroom. The achievement scores in Biology were influenced by the selected variables Sex, Locale and Management of the school when the developed models were implemented in the classroom therefore teachers should take into account the nature of the students, nature of the school before adopting a particular instructional strategy.

The developed models were superior to lecture method in realizing the instructional objectives of Biology. This reemphasizes the need for teachers to attempt discovery learning strategies, memorization strategies and computer based strategies while teaching Biology.

Experts rated Discovery learning superior to both computer based method and memory method in attaining affective and process skills outcomes. Therefore, Discovery learning should be encouraged but ample scope and provision for incorporating transfer of process skills and developing interest, curiosity and appreciating the diversity of nature should be incorporated when implementing memorization strategies and computer based instruction. Encouraging collaborative learning activities when implementing computer based instruction is ideal for taking into account the dehumanizing tendency of computer based instruction.

Teachers rated the developed models superior to lecture method in realizing the instructional objectives of Biology. This implied that teaching strategies that encouraged whole class participation, inquiry, problem solving, group activities, computer based instruction, direct techniques of helping students how to learn need to be enforced by teachers.

The extent of practice of the teachers in these alternative teaching strategies can be ensured if the resources become available in the school for the teaching/learning process and constraints pertaining to successful implementation viz., rigidity of the time table, lack of training of teachers, lack of proper guidelines to teachers, lack of computers and adequate educational software.

Implications of the Study

Secondary education is a very important phase of the educational span of the student. It is during this phase that students need to acquire a meaningful understanding of underlying concepts of natural and scientific phenomenon. As Piaget has remarked students in this stage are in the stage of doing formal operations. It is often a turning point towards the future. It is the secondary education phase that decides a student's future career. Any misconceptions regarding self or the subject can contribute to making the wrong decisions. The student thereby lands in a wrong course embarking on a wrong career. Learning and teaching of science should emphasize the conceptual understanding of science which involves being aware of the evidences that justifies scientific knowledge and having the confidence to apply the knowledge to explain real life phenomenon (Longbottom and Butler :1999).

The findings of the study highlights the need for making secondary Science education process oriented, learner-centered, activity centered, technology- enhanced, multi- learning centered, catering to individual differences and diverse learning needs. Teachers need to be encouraged to direct their teaching towards classroom participation, helping students to learn and making learning a pleasant experience. Multi–learning strategies caters to the learning demands and needs of the majority rather than a few of the group that constitutes the class. It takes care of the concept of individual differences and diverse learning capabilities of a heterogeneous group.

Implications for Pedagogy

Emphasizing process oriented science education calls for innovations in methodologies employed in the classroom. Teachers need to be encouraged to make use of dynamic and activity based learning strategies whereby students indulge in whole class discussions. Instructional strategies like Discovery learning provides ample scope for classroom participation, exchange and sharing of ideas, helps in arousing and sustaining the curiosity and appreciation for the content under discussion. Being a process oriented method it was found to influence the development of process skills like observation, identification, classification, drawing comparisons, conclusions and hypothesis testing etc. All these necessary for development of scientific temper which is one of the vital goals of science education. Memorization strategies give a sense of control to the learning making him aware and competent in use of specific learning/ study habits that help him in the process of learning. Students have found to react positively to instructional strategies that grants them control of the learning process. This contributes to independent learning habits (Norman, 1980). Computer enriched environment exploits the learning potentialities of computers. It can reduce the monotony of the classroom lectures and the overload of Teacher talk. It serves the dictum 'Seeing is believing, believing is knowing, knowing is learning'.

Implications for Teacher Education

It is in the teacher education institutions that prospective teachers are moulded, groomed and fostered. In this context it is necessary that a revamping is done in the Teacher Education scenario. Restructuring of the curriculum emphasizes changes to be made in the content (syllabus) and methodologies (transaction of the curriculum). Teacher Educators need to be trained in use of diverse instructional strategies to meet the demands of the restructured curriculum and goals of Science Education. Student trainees need to be equipped with hands on and minds on experiences in use of various instructional strategies suitable for teaching/learning Science. Student trainees need to be prepared and made competent towards teaching in technologically enhanced learning environments. As part of the teacher education programme it becomes imminent that students attain familiarity of web based learning environments and various aspects of e-learning.

Curriculum developers need to provide guidelines to teachers through handbooks of the possibilities for using and implementing process oriented strategies in the classroom while teaching a particular content. Adequate computers, Educational software for computer assisted instruction needs to be made available in the school for the free use of teachers for the benefit of the students. This also calls for adequate subject teachers competent in use and preparation of educational software.

These goal directed steps will help to make the learning of science meaningful, interesting and relevant.

Suggestions for Further Research

The present study is neither comprehensive nor exhaustive. Various modifications in form and structure are required by further research. Hence some suggestions for further research are presented below:

1. The effectiveness of the developed models viz., (Discovery Learning Model (DLM), Memory Model (MM) and Computer based Model (CBM)) was tested experimentally on only one select topic in Biology at Secondary level. More models on other areas of Biology may be prepared and effectiveness may be tested experimentally for various Topics.
2. The models developed were confined to only one subject viz., Biology. More models may be prepared and effectiveness may be tested experimentally for other subjects also.
3. The effectiveness of the developed models was tested experimentally on only English Medium students at Secondary level. The study can be replicated on students of other Mediums of Instruction (Malayalam, Tamil etc.).
4. The experimental part of the study was confined to students of Standard VIII. The same study can be repeated on students of other age groups and at different levels (Primary, Higher Secondary, Vocational, Higher Education)

5. Similar studies can be conducted to identify the opinion and attitude of students towards Discovery Learning Method, Memory Method and Computer based Method
6. The experimental study was confined to a limited sample (N= 60). The experimental part of the study can be replicated on a larger sample to include other variables (Medium of instruction, Coastal and non-coastal, Tribal and non tribal).
7. The study was confined to schools of Thiruvananthapuram district. The study can be repeated to include other districts also to make generalizations about the effectiveness of Discovery Learning Method, Memory Method and Computer based Method.

Bibliography

Abbott, M. (1990). *Effective Teaching and Learning*. Prentice-Hall India Ltd.

Adamson, J.M. (1997). Cooperative learning with Interactive multimedia. The Effect of Gender and Group Composition on Attitude and Interaction, Ph.D. Thesis. Iowa State University. *Dissertation Abstracts International*, Vol. 58.

Agarwal, R. (1995). A Comparative Study of Conceptual Understanding by Programmed Instruction and Computer- assisted Instruction cited in *Indian Educational Abstracts* issue 4. Jan. 1998, NCERT.

Aguire, A. (1997). The Effects of Cooperative Competitive and Individual Computer Assisted Instruction on Achievement of Middle School Students (Doctoral Dissertation, University of Houston. *DAI*, 58(8).

Ajiwole, G.A. (1991). Effects of discovery and expository instructional methods on the attitude of students to Biology. *Journal of Research in Science Teaching, 28(3).*

Akahori, K. (1988). Evaluation of Educational Computer software in Japan (1): Methods and Results. *Programmed Learning and Educational Technology*, 25(1).

Ali, Salim (1976). *Birds of India and Pakistan*. London: Routledge Pvt. Ltd.

Allen, D. and Anne, L. (1997). The Effects of Computer-based Multimedia. Lecture Presentations on Community College Microbiology Student's Achievement Attitudes and Retention. Ph.D. The University of Texas at Austria. *Dissertation Abstracts International* Vol.

Ambili, S. (1997) Construction and Testing of Discovery Learning Model for Teaching Sets in Mathematics for Std. VIII. Unpublished M.Ed. Thesis. University of Kerala.

Anderson, R.C., Spiro, R.J. and Montague, W.E. (1977). *Schooling and the Acquisition of Knowledge.* Hillsdale: N.J: Erlbaum.

Andrews, J.D.W. (1984). Discovery and Expository learning compared their effects on independent and dependent students. *The Journal of Educational Research, 78(2).*

Anitha, K.M. (1998). Realization of Instructional objectives for learning Biology in Secondary schools of Kerala. M.Ed Dissertation, University of Kerala.

Anyarechi and Marie E.C. (1996). Teaching Science in Nigerian Secondary School using a constructionist model. *Dissertation Abstracts International,* Vol. 58(4).

Arkes, H., Schumacher G. and Gardner E. (1976) Effects of orienting tasks on the retention of Prose material. *Journal of Educational Psychology* 68.

Atkinson, R.C. (1975) Mnemotechnics in Second language Learning. *American Psychologist,* 30.

Atkinson, R.C. and Raugh M.R. (1975) An application of the Mnemonic Keyword Method to the Acquisition of a Russian Vocabulary. *Journal of Experimental Psychology Human Learning and Memory,* 104.

Barker, J. and Tucker, N.R. (1990). *The Interactive Learning Revolution: Multimedia in Education and Training.* New York: Kogan Page.

Barne, J.M. and Nikole (Eds). (1988). *Science Curriculum a Resource Book.* New Delhi: Sage Publications.

Barnett, J.E., Divesta, F.J. & Rogozinst, J.T. (1981). What is learned in note taking? In T.Husen & T.N. Postlethwaithe

(Eds). *The International Encyclopedia of Education*, pp. 1212-1223.

Batchelder, John Stuart(1997). Effects of Computer–assisted Instruction on Male Inmate Maths and Reading Achievement scores. Ph.D. The University of Southern Mississippi. *Dissertation Abstracts International.*

Beck, I., Perfetti, C and McKeown, J. (1982). The effects of long -term vocabulary construction on textual access in reading comprehension. *Journal of Educational Psychology. (75).*

Beena, G.S. (1998) *Preparation and Testing of Discovery Learning Model for Teaching Biology at Primary Level.* Unpublished M.Ed Thesis. University of Kerala.

Bishop (1997) *Learning Strategies in the Classroom.* Hillsdale: N.J: Erlbaum.

Bjorklund, D.F. (Ed) (1990) *Children's Strategies: Contemporary Views of Cognitive Development.* Hillsdale: N.J. Erlbaum.

Bjorklund, D.F., Ornstein P.A. and Haig J.R (1977). Developmental differences in Organization and recall – Training in the use of Organizational techniques. *Developmental Psychology*, 13.

Borland, D.F. & Muir, J.E. (1988). Children's development of free recall memory: remembering on their own, in R. Vasta (Ed), *Annals of Child Development*, (Vol. 5), Greenwich.

Bower, G.H. & Mayer, J. (1985). Failure to replicate mood-dependent retrieval. *Bulletin of the Psychonomic Society, 23.*

Brophy, G.A. (1996). The Effects of Hypermedia on the Comprehension of Science Text among Sixth grade students. PhD. Edinburgh University, *Dissertation Abstracts International. 57.*

Brown, A.l., Bransford, J.D., Ferrara R.A, and Camp ions, J.C. (1983). Learning, remembering and understanding. In

J.H. Flavell & E.M. Markman (Eds). *Handbook of Child Psychology, Vol. 3, Cognitive Development*. New York, Wiley & Sons Pvt Ltd.

Burkman, Thomas A. (1996). An Analysis of the Relationship of Achievement, Attitude and Sociological Element of Individual Learning Style of Students in an Interactive Telecrime. Ed. D.W. Michigan University. *Dissertation Abstracts International*, Vol. 58 (3).

Callahan, J.F. and Leonard, H.C. (1990). *Teaching in the middle and secondary schools*. Maxwell McMillan. International Editions.

Carole, A.B. (1990). Structured versus Discovery Instructional formats for improving concept acquisition by Domain-experienced and Domain-novice Adult learning.

Chadwick, D.K.H. (1997). Computer Assisted Instruction in Secondary Mathematics Classroom- A meta–analysis. Ed.D. Drake University. *Dissertation Abstracts International* Vol.

Chien, Chieng – Chin, (1997). The Effectiveness of Interactive Computer Simulation on College Engineering Student's Conceptual Understanding and Problem–solving Ability Related to Circular Motion. (PhD). The Ohio State University. *Dissertation Abstracts International*, Vol. 57.

Chou, Ya Lun (1981). *Statistical Analysis with Business and Economic Applications*. II Editions. Holt Reinhart and Winston Ltd., New York.

Cieutat, V.J. Stockwell, F.E. & Noble, C.E. (1958). The interaction of ability and amount of practice with stimulus and response meaningfulness in paired-associate learning. *Journal of Experimental Psychology*.

Collis, B. (1984). Manipulating critical variables—A framework for improving the impact of computers in the school environment. In T. Husen & T.N. Postlethwaithe (Eds), *The International Encyclopedia of Education*.

Cramer, D. (1998). *Fundamental Statistics For Social Research.* N. York: Routledge.

Daglish, E.F. (1932). *How to See Birds.* London: J.M. Dent and Sons Ltd.

Daniel, F. (1983). *General Science for Tropical Schools.* London, Oxford University Press.

Dansereau, D.F. (1985). Learning strategy research. In J. Segal, S. Chipman and R. Glase (Eds). *Thinking and Learning Skills,* Vol. I, *Relating Instruction to Research.* Hillsdale, N.J: Erlbaum.

Dansereau, D.F., Collins, K.W., McDonald, B.A., Holley, C.C.D., Garland, J, Dekhoff, G.& Evans, SH. (1979). Development and evaluation of a learning strategy training program. *Journal of Educational Psychology,* 71.

Defneze, Deborah Kay, (1998). The Influence of Computer Use on Student Achievement: A Comparison of Unstructured and Structured Computer Lab Environments, *Dissertation Abstracts International,* Vol. 59.

Delors, J. (1996). *Learning the Treasure Within.* UNESCO Publishing.

Department of Education, Govt of Kerala, Kerala State Syllabus Standard VIII (previous version) and Standard IX (Biology).

Dewey, J. (1959). *Experience of Education.* N. York: McMillan.

Dewey, J. (1951). Experience and Education. In Lee C. Deighton (Ed.). *Encyclopedia of Education.*

Driver, R. (1989). The Construction of Scientific Knowledge in School Classrooms. In Millar, R (Ed.). *Doing Science: Images of Science in Science Education.* London: Palmer Press Lewes.

Dunn, S. & Ridgeway, J. (1991). Computer use during primary

school teaching. A practice survey. *Journal of Computer Assisted Learning, 7,67-79.*

Eggen, P.D., Kauchak, D.P. & Harder, R.J. (1979). *Strategies for Teachers.* Englewood Cliffs: Prentice Hall Inc.

Ekambaranthan, A and A Ananthakrishnan (1982), *A Manual of Zoology (Invertebrata).* Madras: A P H Publishers Pvt Ltd.

Ekambaranthan A and Ananthakrishnan (1982) *A Manual of Zoology (Vertebrata).* Madras: A.P.H. Publishers Pvt. Ltd.

Emex, G.L. (1993). The effects of Guided Discovery Style Teaching and Graphic Calculus in Differential Calculus. *Dissertation Abstracts International,* Vol. 54 (2).

Exemmal, J. (1998). *Construction of certain models for teaching school Botany using Environmental and Ethnic Resources and Testing the Efficacy of Such Models.* PhD Thesis, University of Kerala.

Flavell, J.H., Freidrichs, A.H. & Hoyt, J.D. (1970). Developmental changes in memorization processes. *Cognitive Psychology.*

Fraenkel, J.R. and Wallen, Norman E. (1993). *How to Design and Evaluate Research in Education?* McGraw Hill Inc.New York.

Froebel (1826) On the Education of man. In Lee C. Deighton (Ed.) *Learning.*

Gardner, H. (1987). *Genetics.* N. York: McGraw Hill Publishers.

Gabel, D.L. & Bunce, D.M. (1994). *Research on Problem Solving Chemistry.*

Garrett, H.E. (1973). *Statistics in Psychology and Education.* Vakils, Pfeffer and Simons Pvt. Ltd.

George, K. and Kaplan, D. (1995). A structural model of Parent Teacher influences on science attitudes of eighth graders: Evidence from NELS: 88. As cited in Richard A

Duschl (Ed.). *Science Education*, Vol. 82.

Gruneberg, M. (1992). *Link Word Language System*. Greek: London: Corgi Books.

Gawford, O.G. (1998). An Analysis of the Effects of a Learning Style Seminar and a Computer–assisted Instructional Package on the Academic Achievement of Selected Seminary Students. PhD Smith western Baptist.Theological Seminary. *Dissertation Abstracts International*, Vol. 54(2).

Gibbons, J D. (1971). *Non Parametric Statistical Inferences*. Tokyo: McGraw Hill Kogakusha Ltd.

Good, C.V. (1967). *Dictionary of Education*. N. York: McGraw Hill Publishers Ltd.

Government of India Publication, Ministry of Human Resources Development. *Secondary Education Commission Report*, p. 77.

Government of India Publication. Ministry of Human Resources Development. *Education Commission Report (1964-66)*, p. 76.

Government of India Publication. Ministry of Human Resources Development. *The New Education Policy* (1986).

Government of India Publication. Ministry of Human Resources Development. *Ramamurti Review Committee* (1990-92).

Grant, Andrew Morton, (1998) Verbal and visual learning of science terminology by High School Biology Students PhD Kent. State University. *Dissertation Abstracts International*, Vol. (57).

Hagen, J.W. & Kail, R.V. (1973). Facilitation and Distraction in Short Term Memory. *Child Development*, 44.

Hintzman, D.L. and Summer, J.J. (1973). Long term visual traces of visually presented words. *Bulletin of the* Psychomotor Society, 1.

Hasselhorn, M. (1990). The emergence of strategic Knowledge activation in categorical clustering during retrieval. *Journal of Experimental Child Psychology.*

Hezelbaker, Deborah Jean (1998). A Comparative Study Examining the Effects of Alternative Methods of Teaching Mathematics on Mathematics Achievement and Attitude to Mathematics Comparing the Lecture—Cooperative Learning Method to the Computer assisted Method. Ph.D. The Union Institute. *Dissertation Abstracts International.* 58 (8).

Howe, M.J.A. (1970). Using student's notes to examine the role of the individual learner in acquiring meaningful subject matter. *Journal of Educational Research,* 64.

Holly, C.D., Dansereau, D.F., McDonald, B.A., Garland, J.C., & Collins, K.W. (1979). Evaluation of a hierarchical mapping technique as an aid to prose processing. *Contemporary Educational Psychology,* 4.

Hyman, R.T. (1974). Ways of Teaching. Rutgers University. J B Lippincott Company, N. York.

Jones, G., Jones, M. and Marchington, P. (1990). *Balanced Science,* London: Cambridge University Press.

Joshi, Anuradha and Mahapatra, B.C. (1997) Effectiveness of Computer Software in terms of Reasoning Ability in Science. *Psycho Lingua,* Vol. 27 (1. *Indian Educational Abstracts* Issue No. 5 July 98.

Joyce, B. & Weil, M. (with Showers, B.), (1995). *Models of Teaching.* New Delhi: Prentice-Hall Inc.

Kothari, R.C. (1991). *Research Methodology,* N. Delhi: Himalayan Publishers Ltd.

Kimmel, K.J. (1998). The development and evaluation of Music Mnemonic enhanced Multimedia computer-aided Science Instruction module. *Dissertation Abstracts International,* Vol. 59(2).

Kuo-Newhour, M. (2000). The effects of Visual and Verbal Mnemonics on Learning Chinese characters in Computer based Instruction. Ph D. *Dissertation Abstracts International,* Vol. 60(12).

Lafronza, V.N. (1997). The Interaction of Adult Learning Styles for the Design of Computer Assisted Instruction (CAI). (PhD Georgia, *Dissertation Abstracts International,* 1997 (58 (3).

Leach, C. (1978). *Introduction to Statistics: A Non-Parametric Approach for the Social Sciences,* John Wiley and Sons, N. York.

Lee, Hing–Ling (1997). The Use of Animation as a Tool for Concept learning. PhD Ohio State University. *Dissertation Abstracts International,* Vol. 58 (3).

Lekshmi, A. (2000). *Development of Computer Assisted Lesson on Genetics for Higher Secondary Students.* M.Ed. Dissertation, University of Kerala, Trivandrum.

Levin, J.R. (1981). The Mnemonic 80s Keywords in the classroom. *Educational Psychologist,* 16 (2), 65 – 82.

Lewis, J.E. and Potter, I.C. (1970). *The Teaching of Science in the Elementary School.*

Lindberg, M.A. (1980). "Is Knowledge base development a necessary and sufficient condition for memory development?" *Journal of Experimental Child Psychology,* 30.

Linderman, R.H. (1967). *Educational Measurement.* Illinois: Scott, Fisserman and Company.

Lorayne, H. and Lucas J. (1974). *The Memory Book.* New York: Ballantine Books.

Mayer, R.E. (1980). Elaboration Techniques that increase the meaningfulness of technical prose, An experimental test of the learning strategy hypothesis. *Journal of Educational Psychology* 72.

Mach, M. (1998). A Case Study: Student use of Hypertext in an Elementary School Classroom. University of Minnesota. PhD Thesis *Dissertation Abstracts International,* Vol. 59.

Machado, Patricia Bais (1998). The Effects of Computer – assisted Technology on the Language Acquisition rates of Second language Acquisition of Students. Ed.D, United States International University. *Dissertation Abstracts International,* Vol. 57 (3).

Madhu Mohan, B.S. (1999). *A Comparative Study of the effectiveness of self-study approach and Teacher centered approach in learning Chemistry in standard XI.* Ph.D. Thesis, University of Kerala.

Maya S. (1999). *Preparation and testing of Computer assisted lesson on Tissue system in Biology for Standard VIII.* M.Ed Thesis, University of Kerala.

McClure, P.H. (1996) Computer–related technology use of High school Physics classroom. A case study. (Ed.D.) Virginia Polytechnic Institute and State University, *Dissertation Abstracts International,* Vol. 59(2).

Meera, S. (2000). Relative effectiveness among different modes of Computer Based Instruction in relation to students personality traits. Bharathiar University.

Meerlo, J. (1961). *The Rape of the Mind.* N. York: Grosset and Dunlap.

Metz, K.E. (1991). Development of explanation: incremental and fundamental change in the children's Physics knowledge. *Journal of Research in Science Teachers,* 28(7), 93-127.

Melczarek, R.J. (1997). The Effects of Problem–solving Activities using Dynamic Geometry Computer Software on Readiness for Self directed Learning. *Dissertation Abstracts International,* Vol. 58 (3).

Moon, Jungun (1997). The Design and Evaluation of a Multimedia Computer Assisted Instructional Program Related to Understanding the Mechanics of Open Kinetic Chain University. *Dissertation Abstracts International,* Vol. 53(3).

Mukundan, G. (1995). *Birds of Periyar*. Department of Forest and Wildlife. Govt. of Kerala.

Mulapo, F.G. and Fowler, A. (1987) A study of Chemistry students in Zambia. *J. Res. Sci Teach,* 24 (3).

Myers, K.R. (1999). Topics in discrete Mathematics structures development and treatment of a Computer Multimedia software (Ed D). Colombia University *Dissertation Abstracts International,* Vol. 608).

Nair, G.P.N. (1978). *The impact of creative methods of teaching on the attainment of higher objectives in science.* Unpublished doctoral dissertation, University of Kerala, Trivandrum.

Nair, N C and Leelavathy S, Soundara P N, Arumugan N. *Text Book of Invertebrates*. Nagercoil: Saras Publications.

Nayar, A and Pushpam, K. (2000). Willingness of Secondary school teachers of Biology to use teaching aids. *School Science,* Vol. 36(4), 58-64.

Nayar, A and Shankar, S. (1999). Self-Learning Instructional Materials in the Learning of Biology: An Experimental Study. *School Science,* Vol. 37(1).

NCERT, *Biology Class VIII.*

NCERT, *Biology Class XII.*

Neelakandan, R. (1977). *Birds of Kerala*. New Delhi: Vikas Publishing House.

Neimiec, R.P., Blackwell, C. and Herbert, J.W. (1986). *CAI can be doubly effective*. Phi Delta Kappa, 67.

Norman, D.A. (1980). Cognitive engineering and Education.In

D.T. Juma and F Reif (Eds). *Problem solving and Education.* Hillsdale.

Norman, A.S. and Sprinthall R.C. (1980). *Educational Psychology: A Developmental Approach.* Prentice-Hall India Ltd.

Ohlsen, M.M. (1959). Learner-centered teaching. Cited in Ohlsen (Ed.). *Modern Methods in Elementary Education.* New York: Henry Holt and Company Inc.

Ornstein, P.A., Naus, M.J., & Stone, B.P. (1977). Rehearsal training and developmental differences in memory. *Developmental Psychology,* 13.

Ostle, B. and Malone, C L. (1988). *Statistics in Research: Basic Concepts and Techniques for Research Workers,* 4th Edition. Amey: IOWA State University Press.

Paivio, A. (1979). *Imagery and Verbal Processes.* N. York. Holt, Reinhart and Weinstein.

Paris, S.G. & Oka, E.R. (1986). Children's reading strategies- Metacognition and motivation. *Developmental Review, 6.*

Piaget, J. (1997) Jon Amos Comenius. Cited in Zaghlul Morsy (Ed.), *Thinkers on Education.* UNESCO.

Preece, J and Jones, A. (1992). Transfer with Computer Technology. Cited in Charles Taylor (Ed.), *Science Education and Information Transfer,* Oxford: Pergamon Press.

Prema, S, Nair (1995). *Construction and Testing of Environment Based Models for Teaching Botany at Degree Level.* Unpublished PhD Thesis.

Pressley, M. & Elliott, F.D.J. (1988). What is strategy instructional enrichment and how to study it? Illustrations from Research on children's prose memory and comprehension. In Lee C Deighton (Ed.) *The Encyclopedia of Education.*

Pressley, M., Levin, J.R., & Bryant, S.L. (1983). Memory and strategy instruction during adolescence: When is explicit instruction needed?. In M. Pressley & J.R. Levin (Eds). *Cognitive Strategy Research* (Psychological Foundations). New York.

Pressley, M., & Levin, J.R. (1978). Developmental constraints associated with children's use of the keyword method of foreign language vocabulary learning. *Journal of Experimental Child Psychology*, 26, pp. 359-373.

Pushpa, S. (1999). *A Study of the Use of Teaching Aids by Biology Teachers in Secondary Schools.* Med Dissertation, Sree Sankaracharya University of Sanskrit, Regional Center, Trivandrum.

Raeburn, J.K., Rae Burn, H.A. (with Gratom H M) *Anatomy, Physiology and Hygiene.* London: John Murray (Publishers Ltd).

Ralph Thomas, E.I. & Robinson, H.A. (1972). *Improving Reading on Every Class: A Sourcebook for Teachers.* Boston: Allyn and Bacon.

Rao, R. and Raghavendra, N.I. (1988).An investigation into relative effectiveness of Guided Discovery and Expository Approach of Teaching Mathematics. Buch M.B (Ed.) Fourth Survey of Research in Education, Vol. 1.

Raugh, M.R. and Atkinson R.C., (1975). Learning strategies cited in T. Husen & T.N. Postlethwaithe (Eds).*The International Encyclopedia of Education.*

Raymond, J.O. Connor (1984). *The Growth and Development of Birds.* N. York: John Wiley and sons.

Reder, L.M. and Anderson J.R. (1980) A Comparison of texts and their summaries Memorial Consequences. *Journal of Verbal Learning and Verbal Behavior*, 19.

Rendall, J. (2001). The effectiveness of a Computer Based Instruction program: A comparative study. Ph. D, Temple University, *Dissertation Abstracts International*, Vol. 61(1).

Rickards, J and August G.J. (1975) Generative Underlining Strategies in Prose recall. *Journal of Education Psychology* 67.

Renaud, Chantelle Antoinette (1998). A Use of Computer assisted Instruction in Rural Science Education, Ph.D. The University of Texas at Houston. *Dissertation Abstracts International,* Vol. 59.

Rousseau, J.J. (1911). *Emile,* (Everyman translation, J.M. Dent).

Ryan, E.B. (1981). Identifying and remediating failures in reading comprehension: Toward an instructional approach for poor comprehension. In T.G. Waller and G.E. Blackinnon. (Eds), *Advances in Reading Research.* New York: Academic Press.

Schallert, D. (1982). The significance of Knowledge. A syntheis of research related to schema theory. In W. Otto and S. White (Eds), *Reading Expository Material,* New York: Academic Press.

Schardt, Angela Marie, (1997). A Comparison of English Language and Reading skills of limited English Proficient Students with and without use of Multimedia. CD – ROM literature based software Ed. D University of Texas at Austin.

Schneider, W. Korkel, J. & Weinert, F.E. (1987). *The knowledge base and memory performance. A comparison of academically successful and unsuccessful learners.* Paper presented at the meeting of the American Educational Research Association, Washington D.C.

Selberg, E.M., Neal. L.A. & Vessel, M.F. (1970). *Discovering Science in Everyday Classroom.* London: Addison -Wesley Publishing Company.

Selim, M.A. & Shrigley, R.L. (1983). The group dynamic approach: A socio psychological approach for testing the effect of discovery and expository teaching in the science achievement and attitudes of young Egyptian students. *Journal of Research in Science Teaching,* 20(3).

Shoffner, M.B. (1998). Effects of Instructional Strategies on Emerging technology–based Visual Literacy Instruction-Problem–based learning, Networked Hypermedia-based instruction of Cooperative, Learning strategies. Ph.D Kent State University. *Dissertation Abstracts International,* Vol. 59.

Shepard, R.N. (1967). Recognition memory for words, Sentences and Pictures. *Journal of verbal learning and verbal behaviour* 6.

Soper, R. (Ed) *Biological Science* (1996) London: Cambridge University Press.

Sreelekha, S. and Nayar, A. (1998). The effectiveness of concept attainment model (CAM) in learning Chemistry at secondary level. *School Science,* Vol. 35(3).

Stonier, T.T. (1985). The computer: Most powerful technology ever? In Alloway, B S and Mills, G.M. (Eds) *Aspects of Educational Technology XVIII.* London: Kogan Page.

Vaidyan,V.K. (1989*). Microcomputers in Teaching Physics.* In Asian Regional Conference on Educational Technology Abstracts. AIAET, Kerala Chapter.

Vidyarthi, R. (1968). *A Text Book of Zoology.* Delhi: Himalayan Publishers Pvt Ltd.

Verma P.S. (1985). *Cytology.* New Delhi: S Chand and Company Ltd.

Wellington, J.J. (1981). "What is supposed to happen, Sir?"- Some problems with discovery learning. *School Science Review 63*(222).

Weinstein, C.E., & Mayer, R.E., The teaching of learning strategies. in M.C. Wittrock (Ed), *Handbook of Research on Teaching,* 3rd Edition, NY: Macmillan Publishing Company.

Wingfield, W.A. (1979). *Human Learning and Memory.* New York: Harper & Row.

Williams, G. (1995). *Advanced Biology for You.* London: Stanley Thorne's Publishers Ltd.

Wittrock, M.C. (1978). "The cognitive movement in instruction." *Educational Psychologist,* 13.

Wittrock, M.C. (1974). "Learning as a generative process." *Educational Psychologist,*11.

Worthen, B. (1968). "A study of the discovery and expository presentation: Implications for teaching." *Journal of Teacher Education,* 19, 223-242.

Young, C.V. (1971). *The Magic of a Mighty Memory.* West Nyack NY, Parker Publishing Company.

Young, J.Z. (1983). *The Life of Vertebrates.* Oxford: Clarendron Press.

Zaghlul Morsy (Ed.), (1997). *Thinkers on Education.* Oxford: UNESCO.

Index

V

W

Y

Z